For Brian — partner, paddler, fisherman, naturalist, nurse, cook, mechanic, bee-swatter, proofreader and husband.

NOTE:

The map of Baja California is on page 49. Please note that in each chapter, route maps *follow* route descriptions.

See 1995 Update at the end of the book, following the author's biography, for additional changes and comments for this second printing.

Sea
Kayaking
in
BAJA

Andromeda Romano-Lax

WILDERNESS PRESS
Berkeley

First edition September 1993
Second printing December 1995

Copyright © 1993 by Andromeda Romano-Lax

Photos by Brian R. Lax and A. Romano-Lax
Maps by A. Romano-Lax
Design by Thomas Winnett and Lindsay Mugglestone
Cover design by Larry B. Van Dyke

Library of Congress Card Catalog Number 93-27790
ISBN 0-89997-157-1

Manufactured in the United States of America
Published by Wilderness Press
      2440 Bancroft Way
      Berkeley, CA 94704
      (510) 843-8080

        Write for free catalog

Library of Congress Cataloging-in-Publication Data
Romano-Lax, Andromeda, 1971-
    Sea kayaking in Baja / Andromeda Romano-Lax.
      p.   cm.
    ISBN 0-89997-157-1
    1. Sea kayaking—Mexico—California, Gulf of—Guidebooks.
    2. California, Gulf of (Mexico)—Guidebooks. I. Title.
    GV778.5.R66 1993
    797.1'224'09722—dc20   93-27790
                                  CIP

Contents

Part I: How-to

Chapter 1: Planning A Trip

Chapter 2: Gearing Up and Getting There

Chapter 3: En Route: Kayaking Baja

Part II: The Routes

Chapter 4: The Baja Pacific

Chapter 5: The Northern Cortés

Chapter 6: The Southern Cortés

Appendices

Index

Introduction

Baja has become one of North America's top sea kayaking spots, and for good reason. This peninsula, a crooked finger of land west of mainland Mexico, is tantalizingly close to the United States and yet still surprisingly wild and untamed. Flanked by the Sea of Cortés (or Gulf of California) to the east and the Pacific to the west, it is an 800-mile strip of desert bounded by over 2000 miles of stunning coastline. Much of it remains inaccessible, except by boat. Despite its growing popularity, much of it remains unexplored, except by those adventurers willing to step (or paddle) off the beaten path.

The kayak provides an unparalleled vehicle for exploring this remote and remarkably beautiful coast. With its shallow draft, a kayak can enter any cove, navigate a lonely echoing channel or steer a course through a maze of offshore boulders. It can be transported to almost any launching spot along the peninsula, be hauled out into a cliff niche or pulled above the high-tide line of a beautiful, secluded beach. It is less expensive than a yacht, more unobtrusive and ecologically sound than a motorboat. It can be paddled well and safely, even by the beginner. It is great exercise, a perfect craft for the bird-, whale- and wildlife-watcher, and a good way to burn off the pounds that creep on somewhere near Ensenada.

Planning to kayak a desert coast in a foreign land is a formidable task, however. That strange world, that narrow strip of coast where harsh, unforgiving desert meets fertile sea is a place like no other, with its own secrets and challenges. It is a place that demands, if not worship, humility and prayer to the great Sun-god Huitzilopochtli, at least some good topographical maps and careful, strategic planning.

My own attempts to plan my first Baja kayaking trip didn't get off to a very good start. I was determined to see the "other Baja": the Baja beyond Highway 1, the coastal Baja of hidden beaches and desert islands and oases. But I was plagued by a few logistical problems.

First, I didn't know much about coastal Baja; few guidebooks even mentioned the places I wanted to visit. Second, anyone I asked for advice kindly referred me to tour groups I could join, and strictly cautioned me against doing anything independently. My enthusiastic search for information was extinguished in an avalanche of glossy brochures, with impressive fee lists and meticulous itineraries, all put out by adventure travel companies who seemed determined to take the "adventure" out of my travels.

Most experts flatly told me I couldn't do it on my own. So, as the story goes, I did. And I'm not the only one. While kayaking Baja, I met many other people of all ages who do day trips, week-long tours or epic expeditions without ever alerting the press or requiring a full entourage of experts paddling behind them.

I made a lot of mistakes, and stumbled into some incredible experiences. Through trial and error (heavy on the error) I gathered information that would have made my own first foray into Baja kayaking more enjoyable and safer.

Since that first trip, I have fallen in love with sea kayaking, not only as a sport but as a lifestyle and a way to see the world. I've tried paddling other places (currently I live and kayak in Nova Scotia) but so far nothing compares to Baja.

This book, the result of that first trip and the many that followed, does not cover every inch of coastline or divulge every secret spot, but it will help you plan your own tours and perhaps find your own favorite, secret spots. It describes a variety of routes, 15 in all, which provide a sampling of the Baja coast's diverse environments: from placid bays and sheltered lagoons to pounding surf and long stretches of sheer, cliffy shore. It also answers some questions that are exceedingly important en route: how to adapt your kayaking skills to Baja's waters, where to obtain supplies, what to expect from the weather, and who to turn to in case of emergency. I have tried to include enough details to make planning, enjoying and surviving a trip possible, even for the absolute beginner; but not so many details that there is nothing left to discover.

Kayaking Baja is often associated with incredible, triple-digit mileage trips, but there is an alternative to such expeditions: there is exploration. Expeditions have their place; they teach us something about human resiliency and endurance. But explorations, often smaller-scale and more leisurely paced, teach us about the world, infuse us with awe, and are within the capabilities of far more people.

For all these reasons, I have written this book for the explorer first, the expeditioner second. I have included no route over 60 miles (perhaps even that is too long!) and I have chosen many routes that are more in the 20-mile range. You may of course string several of them together and do some hefty mileage indeed, but I nonetheless hope you will leave a little room for the unexpected. If a pod of dolphins surrounds your kayak, you'll probably forget all about the mileage you intended to do that day and follow them in circles; backwards if need be. You'll probably store this book hastily in your map case, forget the route description, and wander far, far off course. Good.

Chapter 1

Planning a Trip

So, it's happened. You saw a photo of brightly colored kayaks floating on shimmering turquoise waters, or of a campsite set up on a cacti-studded isle. You listened to a friend tell tales about the Vermilion Sea, as the Cortés was once called; a place that has drawn explorers, pirates, profiteers and adventurers for centuries. Or perhaps you have your own memories of the Baja coast, and you're looking for a few new spots to launch your kayak sometime in the future. The intricacies of planning a private south-of-the-border kayaking trip may seem daunting. This chapter will help.

What Kind of Person Kayaks Baja?

"Loco" may be the first word that comes to mind, but of course that's not true. Taking a small craft into the open sea only seems "crazy" to those people who don't realize how seaworthy a kayak really is—almost always, those who have never paddled one. Sure, it's fun to get stares from local fishermen, who like to pantomime drowning and shark attacks in an attempt at communication. But chances are, if you ask them, they may remember their grandparents going out in *cayucos* or *kayakas*, before the days of the panga, the small motorized boat most of Baja's small-scale fishermen now use.

In reality, all kinds of people currently kayak Baja. Most of them are tourists, though some American residents already living in Baja keep a kayak handy for short trips. I've heard of kayakers as young as 8 and as old as 85, though most seem to be in the 30–60 range. One kayaker suggested that younger people don't flock to the sport because it's too sedate; I think the initial investment in equipment and transport keeps younger adventurers away, though that may be changing. In any case, age isn't an issue in Baja. Regardless of age, there are probably kayakers older or younger than you; and after weeks of paddling without seeing a soul, your first encounter may be with a retiree out for his or her evening paddle.

In terms of experience, there is a similarly broad range. World-class expedition kayakers and novices alike have gotten their start in the Sea of Cortés, where most Baja paddling takes place. When I first launched at San Felipe, the northernmost city on Baja's eastern coast, my only time spent in a kayak had been in a YMCA pool.

Many people who kayak for the first time are surprised to find that it isn't as difficult as they expected. Unlike riding a bicycle or ice skating, a beginner can manage (in this case, paddle) quite competently within minutes. After catching their breaths and gliding a few feet across the water, the first words out of most of my friends' mouths have been: "It's so easy!"

There's more to kayaking than simply staying afloat, however. An inefficient paddlestroke leads to aching muscles, fatigue or injury. More advanced paddlestrokes become necessary to deal with waves and wind. Navigation and map-reading are additional skills to be acquired. Launching and landing in all but the most perfect conditions take a lot of practice and experimentation. Rescues and emergency situations are taxing even for the expert.

In other words, kayaking can be initiated quite easily, but mastering it requires much more. In this regard, books and articles don't contribute as much as experience. Sometimes you have to paddle for a while first before you can even understand the specific skill or problem an article is describing.

I think kayaking Baja is a great way to get that experience, as long as certain precautions are taken. For that reason, I don't think most routes in the Sea of Cortés or more sheltered routes on the Pacific are necessarily "off limits" for novices. On the other hand, some routes which are easy and safe on one day can be challenging or even life-threatening on another. Very often, weather and local conditions more than the paddler's experience level will dictate a given route's difficulty, and the most important skill to acquire is knowing when you should stay on land to wait for bad conditions to pass.

What Kind of Trip?

From a 2-mile paddle on the lazy Río Rosalía, to a 20-mile island hopping tour in Bahía de Los Ángeles, to what some consider their "dream trip": a 670+-mile voyage from San Felipe to La Paz, there are many levels at which one may kayak Baja.

Whether you are planning a vacation, a tour or an expedition, you may be deliberating not only on trip style and pace, but also philosophy. Why are you doing this? To make miles and challenge yourself to the limit; or to see wildlife; or to seek out a paradisiacal spot as quickly as possible and stay there until your supplies run out? All these goals are valid, but not all can be achieved simultaneously.

Pace, in particular, is worthy of a little reflection. One of the best-known books about paddling Baja is *Keep It Moving* by Yalerie Fons. In response to her title, does anyone ask simply, "Why?" A lot of kayakers, myself included, can't look at a map of Baja without envisioning attempting the whole thing, nonstop, expedition style; but we have to remind ourselves that there are tradeoffs inherent in that kind of trip.

A season spent kayaking the whole length of the peninsula is an incredible life-changing event. But make no mistake; those who do it usually paddle about 25 miles per day, and don't make landfall often. They may paddle the entire coast, but they often see very little of it. They pass up fish camps, lovely beaches, even entire towns. "No time, no time," they contend, because they must make it to the next campsite highlighted on their maps.

Part of this mad rush is due to the coast's configuration: one must make it past a set of cliffs or to the next town or oasis within a set number of days or risk running out of water and supplies. Part of the rush is due to the fact that people have lives waiting back home: spouses, children, jobs. Long-distance kayakers often see no alternative to backbreaking, written-in-stone schedules. Some think kayaking is only about paddling; not about pausing, investigating, resting, contemplating, celebrating, or arriving.

In practice, my kayaking style is a little different. Lest I fool you into thinking that my slower pace is due only to personal philosophy, however, let me confess a few things. Sometimes I'm just tired: my back aches, my arms feel like spaghetti. Sometimes I'm afraid: the waves look ominous, the wind is strong, and I have a bad feeling in my bones. And sometimes I feel lazy; Mexico is not such a bad place to feel lazy.

All this is said on behalf of those who don't want to do nonstop paddling. Go ahead, spend several more days on Isla Espíritu Santo. Forget long distance; spend a month exploring every cove and rocky point and islet in Bahía Concepción; you'll probably discover more than any kayaker before you has. It is not too late to discover new places; to camp on uncharted beaches and circumnavigate unnamed isles. If you'd rather not go far, spend more time getting to know one small area on exceedingly intimate terms. It strikes me that kayak touring, done in this way, enables one to do what Hokusai did: gather many views of one place, from every perspective, every angle, and come to know something of its essence.

In the end, every kind of trip has its own rewards. I find more leisurely trips invigorating, but I'm still secretly (almost shamefully) inspired by killer, long-distance expeditions. No two trips, or two kayakers for that matter, are identical. Some people like to "keep it moving"; some people like to stop and set up camp at every beautiful spot along the way. Everyone has their own preferred pace and style.

Commercial Trips

This book is written primarily for those who want to plan their own trips, but commercial trips or tours deserve mention. In my mind, the best thing about them is also the worst thing: they do most of the work for you. For me, a great part of the fun, adventure and challenge starts as soon as the maps and scratch pads come out. Figuring out where to go, what to see, how to overcome obstacles and handle the logistics creatively is as much a part of kayaking as the paddling. There may be more risk and work in planning one's own trip, but also greater reward. It is an incomparable experience to be sitting on an island thousands of miles from home, several miles offshore, and to think: I got here. Back home, long after the tan fades, there is a serenity imparted from the knowledge that you made it happen.

To be fair, though, some people wouldn't experience sea kayaking if they had to do it all. For them, it's a great relief to be told where to go and to see what the brochure promises. Additionally, commercial trips have some other potential advantages. If you don't know anything about kayaking, they're safer. If you do know something about kayaking, you may be able to pick up even more skills with personalized instruction from your tour leader. Not having to buy, rent or transport kayaks and equipment on your own can be a time- and money-saver. You may not have to cook or set up camp. Large, organized trips offer a great way to meet people. Experienced tour leaders often know a specific area well, and can point out plants and wildlife better than any guidebook. They can also answer a lot of questions. Having fellow group members nearby can be encouraging and can help make the time pass more quickly. In general, if your image of a great kayak trip is pulling up to a beach, being handed an ice-cold beer, and not having any responsibilities until the next day's paddle, you are most likely envisioning a commercial kayaking trip.

Those are some of the pro's and con's. Keep in mind that each touring company has its own unique personality. Some emphasize self-sufficiency, and may make you do a lot of the work of setting up and taking down camp. Some emphasize comfort, and include panga escorts to carry the bulk of equipment as well as any tired or injured paddlers. Tours may or may not emphasize nature observation en route. Some have specific themes, such as all women, or the observation of a specific animal or event. You might also inquire if trip schedules include free time for snorkeling and exploring on your own. Other questions to ask: How many miles per day? How many paddlers and leaders per group? Average experience of each paddler? Single or double kayaks?

Self-Planned Trips: How Fast, How Long, How Far?

To start, the basic speed at which a moderately skilled kayak paddles is just over 3 miles per hour. (Although "knots" and "nautical miles" are ususally used in sailing and boating, this book will use "miles per hour" and "statute miles" in referring to speed and distance. For reference, 1 knot = 1.15 statute miles per hour. This difference is negligible when discussing paddling speed, but significant when discussing high wind speeds or when translating long distances from nautical miles to statute miles.)

That average is helpful in computing daily mileages, but don't take it too seriously. If you know your own average, good. If you don't, you may not have paddled much yet and may go a bit slower. In any case, speed depends not only on changing conditions like wind and waves, but also how many breaks you take, whether you stop paddling periodically to snap pictures, set out a fishing line, etc.

Daily distance is affected by many variables, beyond both speed and simple endurance. Even if you are going strong and paddling rapidly, that wind that picks up nearly every afternoon may force you to land. Even if you're going strong and conditions are perfect, you may stop short of your limit because you've reached the last good camping spot for the next several miles. Even if you're going strong, the sea is glassy calm and there are great camping beaches as far as the eye can see, you may stop because there are other pursuits tempting you: swimming, snorkeling, hiking and so on.

Delays and distractions aside, keep in mind that endurance is not defined only by how long your arm muscles are willing to pump. On my first trips, I found that my legs got cramped and my back got sore before my arms tired, though this problem diminished with time. Additionally, as with all long-distance sports, the mental tedium of repetitive paddling may limit your daily mileage long before physical exhaustion occurs.

To generalize, a beginner might find 5 miles per day comfortable, while an expert might be able to handle 25 miles or more. 10–15 miles is all I care to do on any given day. For me, this translates to about 3–5 hours of kayaking when conditions are good, which I stretch out into a full day by stopping at intervals to hike, snorkel, eat, or rest in a shady niche.

Every few days on a long trip, you should expect a day either so bad (fatigue, illness or winds that prevent paddling) or so good (a cove, island or village you just don't want to leave) as to make that day's departure impossible. For me, this usually seems to occur one day for every three.

To conclude, there are people who stick to a schedule perfectly and paddle through (and past) anything and everything. They're not much fun, though. Unexpected delays and distractions, both welcome and unwelcome, conspire to foil your plans and make your trip more interesting. Leave yourself a little unscheduled time each day, and a few entirely unscheduled days each week.

Longer Distance Trips

As trips get longer, in both time and distance, a few final variables arise. One of these is the amount of equipment, and therefore weight, that you'll be hauling over the waves. The longer you'll be away, and the farther into the unknown you'll venture, the more you'll need to carry in the way of water, supplies and emergency gear. In some places you can re-supply en route; in other places you must bring absolutely everything with you for the whole trip. Kayaks are prodigiously generous with the amount of space they offer, with approximately three to four times the capacity of a backpack. Nonetheless, keep in mind that moving extra weight over extra distance requires a geometrically increasing level of effort.

Fatigue factors into this equation as well. Although even the unfit novice can sometimes paddle surprisingly far for a day or two out of gumption alone, fatigue comes stalking him or her down on the days that follow. Speed and endurance will dwindle from that point on, faster than new muscles can be built.

Planning plenty of rest days alleviates this problem, partly. Depending on how far you're going and where, you may not have the option of resting *too* long, however. Certain stretches are so remote that unless you can make good, consistent daily mileage, you may risk running out of water before you can make it to the next well-populated area.

Acclimation Periods

Whether you paddle a few miles or a few hundred, spend all your time in the cockpit or lounging on the beach, you will find your body (and mind) needs time to adapt to your new environment.

Heat and sun are the most integral aspects of this environment, especially during the hottest times of the year, when temperatures can exceed 110°F. A human requires approximately 5 to 7 days to become heat-acclimated. After that, the body can cool itself more efficiently and is less prone to electrolyte imbalance. High temperatures are aggravated by hard exercise, so don't plan on trying for maximum performance until you've adapted. Even if you're taking it easy, drink plenty of water, and be alert for signs of heat cramps, heat exhaustion or sunstroke.

Sunburn is also a serious risk, especially if you're fair-skinned and intent on wearing a bikini or a bathing suit. Even if you smear on the strongest sunscreen on the market, you will probably burn. Covering up helps, but it's hard to keep everything covered when you're wet and active. The sea acts as an enormous reflector and focuses every ray of the Baja sun on your exposed skin. Particularly in the beginning, you may want to limit your daily time in the kayak for this reason alone.

More will be said on heat and sun later, but they are mentioned here because they will affect how many days your trip will require and how far you'll be able to go. If you won't be in Baja long enough to acclimatize, you shouldn't plan too many miles per day, since a good part of each day will need to be spent recuperating in the shade. New foods, increased physical activity and other changes in your daily routine will pose the same requirement.

Not all adaptations are physical. There are also mental and cultural considerations to keep in mind as you're planning your trip. I'm not fond of cultural cliches, but some persist because they contain an element of truth, and one of these is the notion of "Baja time."

As in many places south of the border and around the world, time does indeed operate a little differently in Baja. If you know any Spanish, you're probably already familiar with *mañana* (tomorrow) and *un momentito* (a small moment) or *un rato* (a while), the latter of which is suggested by the positioning of index finger and thumb about one inch apart.

Paddle as quickly as you may, set up and take down camp as efficiently as you are able, you will still run into the effects of Baja time at some point in your trip. You may be in a rush, but if you step foot in a camp or town where no one else is, be prepared.

During one trip, for example, my partner and I stopped at a camp in hopes of restocking supplies. There was one restaurant, but no store. We asked to buy some basics from the owner: rice, limes, sugar. She said "yes" immediately, but appended this with "un rato." We waited "un rato," which in this case meant 3 days. A party was in the works, and parties can (and probably should) take precedence over anxious, harried kayakers. The wait was fun, especially since we got to attend the party that was essentially holding us hostage. As soon as the last broken bottles and confetti were cleared away, we were sold the supplies we needed and headed south again.

If you don't already have your own anecdotes to illustrate this phenomenon, you probably will by the time you return from your trip. Really lucky paddlers with plenty of time to spare usually end up forgetting what day it is, or how long they've been away. I'm most happy when my only clock is set to the moon; just as long as I can keep track of the tides, I do fine.

Where To Go?

Time to start ogling those maps. This can be the most exciting part of trip planning, especially if you're not familiar with Baja. Start at the top of the peninsula and paddle south? (If you have unlimited time and money.) Throw darts at the map? (Always an option.) Pick the most exotic-sounding port and launch there? (Inevitably Mulegé, in my opinion.) If you'd prefer a more methodical, informed approach, read on . . .

First, a brief look at geography. Baja California is one of the world's longest peninsulas, 800 miles from north to south, flanked by two very different bodies of water: the Sea of Cortés (or Gulf of California) to the east and the Pacific Ocean to the west. A trickle of the Colorado River forms the delta at the Sea of Cortés's northern limit. Separating the peninsula from mainland Mexico, the Cortés is more sheltered than the Pacific and dotted with islands, making it the primary locale for kayaking. Make no mistake, people have kayaked the entire Pacific coast as well; but for pleasure kayaking, only a few parts (primarily bays and lagoons) are of interest.

The Baja peninsula itself is dominated by several mountain ranges which form an almost continuous spine from north to south: the Sierra de Juárez, Sierra San Pedro Mártir, Sierra de la Giganta and Sierra de la Laguna. Most of the peninsula is desert, receiving less than 10 inches of rainfall a year. Some areas may go for several years at a time without receiving any rain at all. The exception is the northwest corner of Baja, near Ensenada, which receives more rainfall and is closer in climate to San Diego than to the rest of Baja.

Generally, the northern stretches of the Cortés experience the greatest extremes: cool in winter, but fiery hot in summer. The southern stretches are slightly less hot in summer with a bit more humidity. All along the Pacific coast damp winds and fogs contribute to a milder climate, even where actual rains are rare.

Mountains and deserts aside, Baja's most important feature is its main highway, Highway 1. Officially dedicated in 1973, it carved a snaking path through rock and rubble, opening up a vast wilderness. In areas where it moves inland, such as in the middle of the peninsula and farther south, between Loreto and La Paz, the coast is left largely unreachable and untouched, except by boat, bush plane and burro. A few smaller highways and many poorly maintained roads also wind through the peninsula, but Highway 1 reigns supreme. You can't see much of Baja, or even drive to your launching spots, without traveling its jagged course. And you can't help but notice its presence nearby while paddling: where asphalt kisses the coast, tamale vendors, RVs and tourist motels abound; where the road can't reach, there are only empty beaches or lonely cliffs looming overhead.

Baja is divided into two states, Baja California Norte and Baja California Sur, most of the population residing in the northern state. Tijuana, with an estimated population of 750,000, accounts for just under half of Baja's total population. The rest is concentrated primarily in the cities of Ensenada and Mexicali, also near the border; as well as La Paz, the capital city of Baja California Sur. A short spur of inhabited and well-visited coast stretches between Santa Rosalía, Mulegé and Loreto in the middle of the southern state. Between these extremes, the border cities of the north, the capital city of the south and a few short stretches of developed land, there are great tracts of uninhabited coast.

Ultimately, where you'll decide to paddle will probably depend on how much time you have, how far you're willing to drive (or fly) to get to the starting point of your kayak trip, and what you're hoping to do and see. A look at a map reveals where Highway 1 meets the coast, making it most accessible. A review of the routes section of this book reveals what features can be found at selected destinations. Most features and activities, such as whale-watching, snorkeling, island-hopping and beach-bumming, are available in more than one location. For example, many people believe that they must go to Bahía Magdalena, on the Pacific in Baja's southern state, to see whales. Actually, there are great opportunities for whale-watching on the sunnier Sea of Cortés as well, especially near Loreto in the south and Bahía de Los Ángeles in the north.

There are great kayaking spots near and far: the starting point for this book's first route, Punta Banda and the Islas de Todos Santos, is only a 2½-hour drive from the border. The starting point for the farthest south route, Isla Espíritu Santo, is at least a 3-day drive: (Flights to Loreto and La Paz, in Baja California Sur, shorten the pre-kayak part of your trip if you're planning to join a commercial tour or rent kayaks in Loreto.)

Finally, don't forget that you can change your mind about where to go after you're south of the border. The narrowness of the peninsula makes it easy to jump from one climate or weather system to another in less than a day's drive. If it's too chilly on Punta Banda on the Pacific, you can shuttle over to San Felipe and bask in the hot, dry climate of the northern Cortés.

When to Go?

Whenever you can. Truth is, most people plan their kayak trips around other priorities, such as vacation time off from work or school. The good thing about Baja is that it does offer year-round paddling opportunities. The only time of year when kayaking is arguably impractical on the Cortés side, due to extreme temperatures, is mid-summer. Coincidentally, that is the time of year when I've logged most of my miles.

With fewer fellow tourists on the beaches or islands, and a white-hot sun glaring down on a warm-to-the-touch sea, Baja seems even more the unconquerable, elusive land of extremes that has daunted men for so long. Of course, it's also damn hot.

In general, to enjoy the most comfortable temperatures, kayak in late spring or late fall: April and October are particularly good months. To avoid crowds, try early summer: June is hot, but not unbearable. To see whales and birds on the Pacific, paddle in the winter. To see them on the Cortés, spring and early summer are good times. A more complete rundown on the seasons follows.

December–March

A mild, sunny climate beckons kayakers who have the winter blahs. Persistent winter northerly winds dictate caution and flexibility, however. Winter storm fronts bringing cold temperatures and wind from the southeast or southwest are also common on the Pacific. The northern reaches of the Cortés and the Pacific can still be a bit chilly, with both air and sea surface temperatures in the 50°s. Farther south on the Cortés, near Loreto and La Paz, temperatures are in the 60°s and 70°s. The gray whale arrives at Bahía Magdalena to calve and breed from December to March, instigating a flurry of whalewatching activity. Winter birdwatching in San Quintín and Bahía Magdalena is excellent. Many commercial kayaking trips operate at this time of year; particularly in Bahía Magdalena but also on Isla Espíritu Santo, you may see others on the route.

April–May

Avoid Easter Week (Semana Santa) if at all possible, especially in San Felipe and Ensenada; crowds swarm.

Northerlies start petering out in May, and temperatures ranging from the 70°s up to the 90°s make kayaking very comfortable. Seabird nesting activity starts up in winter, and is in full swing by spring. This is a good time to see birds in the Cortés, but also a time to be particularly careful about disturbing them; some island campsites and stopping sites should be avoided altogether.

June–August

If you can bear the heat of midsummer, you get the reward: many beaches and islands all to yourself. The northern Cortés is the hottest, with temperatures sometimes exceeding 110°. Farther south, temperatures are less severe, but the sea water can be a little too warm to be refreshing on the hottest days. Winds are generally weakest and more variable. In late summer and early fall, tropical storms visit the peninsula. Evening breezes in the La Paz area keep summer nights comfortable.

Tourists are less common, and even residents occasionally pack up and leave for the summer. Curiously, European visitors don't seem to mind the heat; long after Americans fold up their lawn chairs and leave Bahía Concepción, for example, the Europeans are still sunning and clamming. Bioluminescence lights up the sea, particularly in the middle Cortés regions. Near Loreto, the quest for tuna and dorado heats up as well.

If it's too hot on the Cortés, the Pacific is still comfortable. Cool temperatures and fewer visitors make Bahía Magdalena and San Quintín good spots; the Punta Banda and Islas de Todos Santos route also enjoys a mild summer climate.

September–November

Tropical storm season lasts until early October. Temperatures drop off quickly in October and November: down to the 70°s and 80°s. Commercial trips start up, particularly to Isla Espíritu Santo; you'll probably encounter others on the route.

Communicating

How much Spanish does a visitor to Baja need to know? Many guidebooks reassure readers that English is spoken nearly everywhere. Everywhere that tourists commonly frequent, perhaps. Off the beaten path, however, in smaller towns and camps along the coast, there are plenty of people who do not speak a word of English. The fact that knowing Spanish will make a trip easier and more enjoyable can't be denied.

Of course, as in most places, any small effort helps. The goal, after all, is not fluency, but communication. Especially in the smallest coastal communities, you may find that arriving by small boat speaks for itself. Residents often assume that you're not like the "average tourist." The most basic, piecemeal effort to speak some Spanish will confirm this assumption.

Chapter 2

Gearing Up and Getting There

Having planned your trip, including where you're going and what type of kayaking you'd like to do, you are now ready to gear up. Fortunately, there are plenty of great books available on such basic topics as selection of kayaks, kayaking accessories, and camping equipment (See Appendix B). To avoid unnecessary duplication, this chapter will review the basics only briefly, except for those gear needs and suggestions that are uniquely relevant for the Baja kayaker. This chapter will also review what supplies should be purchased stateside and what can be bought in Baja, as well as final pre-trip preparations to be made. A section at the end of this chapter will provide information on how to get to the Baja coast and finally get your paddling underway.

Kayaks: Buying and Renting

There are a great number of kayak models in all shapes, sizes, materials and price ranges. Sorting them out will require some basic research on your part. Here are a few hints: a river kayak and a sea kayak are different creatures entirely, and Kevlar is not a distant planet. If I've lost you, check out Appendix B again. Read one of the kayak "bibles," such as John Dowd's book, *Sea Kayaking: A Manual for Long-Distance Touring,* or one of the wonderful newer primers such as Randel Washburne's *The Coastal Kayaker: A Complete Guide to Skills, Gear and Sea Sense.* Visit a kayak shop, symposium or local club meeting to see the various makes and models in living color. Just to whet your appetite, be aware that there are double kayaks as well as singles, kayaks that fold up for ease of travel or inflate once you've arrived, and kayaks that are open-topped to encourage snorkeling, splashing and other warm-water pursuits. Even if you plan to rent, not buy, you'll want to discover the great variety that is available.

What boat is best for Baja? I prefer a basic, stable, roomy touring model made of roto-molded polyethylene—what some kayakers call a "bleach bottle"—because it's cheap and can take all the abuse I've given it: dropping it off buildings (once), dragging it over volcanic boulders (twice) and banging it around during off-road desert transport (countless times). I've also enjoyed using an open-top model in warmer, more sheltered waters such as Bahía Concepción, where off-kayak snorkeling and clamming are the craft's raison d'être. I've paddled and envied other Baja aficionados' fiberglass kayaks; more expensive, these are nonetheless sleeker, swifter and reportedly more watertight. In summary, there is no one right boat; your budget and your intended usage of the craft will decide.

Once you've scoped the market, you may decide to buy. Keep in mind that second-hand kayaks are frequently available through shops and club newsletters. In all cases, sit in it, try it out, and find out what it would take to repair it during a trip.

Kayak rentals

Renting is an option, especially if you don't want to transport your kayak all the way to the border. Keep in mind that some shops will not rent to inexperienced kayakers. All of the rentals listed below are subject to change, and new ones will no doubt spring up as demand increases.

On the U.S. side, rentals are currently available at Southwest Sea Kayaks, 1310 Rosecrans, San Diego CA 92106; (619) 222-3616. Southwest Sea Kayaks is a great all-around resource. Not only do they allow you to transport rentals into Baja, but they can sell you all the other gear you'll need and even give you advice on where to go. Ed Gillet, an expedition kayaker who paddled to Hawaii, runs the store with his wife Katie. Their shop newsletter has information on additional lessons and tours they offer, as well as some used kayak deals.

Renting in Mexico is a little more sporadic. Very limited rentals are available in Loreto at Deportes Blazer, Hidalgo No. 18, Loreto B.C.S., Mexico; Phone 011-526-833-0006. Don't expect much additional gear or advice to go with those kayaks. This is a bare-bones operation.

At Playa Santispac, just south of Mulegé, limited rentals are available through Baja Tropicales, Apartado Postal 60, Mulegé B.C.S., Mexico; Phone 011-526-853-0019 or Fax 3-03-63. Baja Tropicales, run by Roy Mahoff and Becky Aparicio, operates out of a palapa on the shore of Bahía Concepción and also offers tours (including inexpensive half-day trips) and instruction.

Some kayakers have been able to rent the basics (although with little instruction and few extras) in Bahía de Los Ángeles. That operation has just recently changed ownership; but if you're in the area, keep an eye out for rentals to start up again.

Kayaking Accessories

I wince to think of the first time I went shopping for kayaking accessories. Walking into a canoe and kayak shop, clutching a credit card between nervous, sweaty fingers, I faced the shop's owner Clint Eastwood-style and told him, "Outfit me." Having found a perfect customer, the owner complied by loading my arms with every gadget ever invented for a kayak expedition. Some pieces of equipment I recognized from articles, books and brochures; other things I feebly tried to return, inconspicuously, to the store's shelves.

The man was actually very helpful, but how was I to be sure which pieces of equipment were essential, which were optional, and which were trivial? Consider these things before you shop. Do your research, make a list, don't buy any extras you won't even be able to fit into your kayak, and certainly don't bother with anything you don't know (or won't be able to learn) how to use. Extra gadgets are just dead weight if you're not familiar with their use and care.

In addition to the packing checklist at the end of this chapter, consider these tips:

Lifejacket: You're more likely to actually wear it if it's comfortable, not too long in the torso (you'll probably be hot enough without extra coverage) and doesn't chafe. A plastic zipper is preferable.

Drysacks: Drysacks, in all shapes and sizes, and additional back-up plastic bags and Ziplocs® (which are difficult to buy in Baja) are essential. Keeping water, salt, sand and excess sun away from gear is a never-ending battle. Camping stoves corrode, tent poles peel and break, batteries bleed, camera equipment dies, clothes reek and food becomes inedible unless you protect it all very carefully. Don't rely on sealed bulkheads to keep all water out; bag and double-bag.

In buying drysacks, choose a variety of sizes for greater packing flexibility. Clear-colored drysacks are particularly useful: you can find that can-opener or that snake-bite kit with a minimum of frantic scrounging.

Sprayskirt: This is not as critical in Baja, particularly in the Sea of Cortés, as in colder-water areas. After all, on hot days you will often enjoy water splashing into your lap. On colder days or in high wave conditions you will find one necessary, however.

Boat repair kit: Most repair materials are not available in Baja. Though you may be able to improvise later, bring what you can. A roll of duct tape should be included in this kit; it will do wonders.

Navigation and Safety Equipment

Compass: On-deck compasses are easier to read at sea, while hand-held compasses are essential for exploration on land. Depending on the nature of your trip, you will want to bring either or both. Remember that as wild as Baja's coast is, its interior is wilder. Anyone who tries to abort a kayak trip by wandering into the desert without a compass, maps and water is in danger.

Tide tables: Baja's tides, particularly in the northern Cortés, are phenomenal (up to 22 feet, in fact) and it's difficult to kayak or set up camp without consulting a table. Tide tables for the Cortés and the Pacific can be ordered from the Map Centre (see Appendix C).

Nautical charts, topographical maps: Most boaters rely on nautical charts. I find topographical maps equally important. Kayak touring is, after all, a unique activity, taking place in a narrow coastal zone which is equal parts land and sea. It is rarely enough to know about water depths and the presence of offshore rocks; one must also possess additional shoreline or even inland information in order to find good campsites, plan hikes, or take compass readings.

Unfortunately, in *both* maps and charts, coverage of Baja is still sketchy. Some charts are inaccurate; many more are out of print or hard to find. As for maps, the Mexican Government puts out a good topo series, but is currently updating some, and in the interim not offering them for sale. Additionally, many of the topos don't include information on offshore islands.

In general, nautical charts are put out by the U.S., Great Britain and Mexico (the latter of which are generally copies of U.S. charts). These can be ordered from the Map Centre or New York Nautical Instruments (See Appendix C). Topographical maps are put out by the Mexican Government, in both a 1:50,000 and a 1:250,000 series. These can be ordered from Map Centre, Wide World of Maps, and many other U.S. map stores.

The best strategy for trip planning is to order indices from one of the stores listed above, which will tell you which maps are currently in print and in stock. This should be done well in advance of your trip.

If no store has what you want, try alternative sources. Fellow kayakers, sailors and boaters may have those maps and charts you're missing. Computer bulletin boards can offer a way to locate rare maps.

Finally, the *Baja Topographic Atlas Directory*, a complete atlas published by *Baja Explorer Magazine*, can be ordered for $28 (see Appendix C). Be warned, however, that this large atlas does not show as much shoreline detail as the Mexican topos; doesn't show major islands such as Isla Carmen, Isla Espíritu Santo and the Todos Santos islands; and is far too large to carry in a kayak. It does make a good general reference, however.

Safety items: Flares, airhorn, whistle, mirror (for signalling) and extra yellow rope for towing are all necessary. I mention them here as an excuse to include this warning: none of them are failproof. In Baja's remote areas, there may be no one within range to see, hear or respond to your signals. Even within short distances of land and people, these devices can be fallible. The last time I tried using my airhorn, I discovered it had leaked and no longer worked; when I blew my whistle, I realized that even my partner couldn't hear it over the wind and the waves. For these reasons, don't rely on only one method of signalling, try out devices when possible and be aware of their limitations, and always be aware of your distance from the next camp or town.

Camping Equipment

In general, evaluate camping equipment not so much on the basis of weight, as you might for backpacking, but on its ability to withstand sand, sun, salt and water. The kayak can hold an impressive amount of cargo: everything from basic survival gear to deluxe amenities such as wine or candles, if you're so inclined. But at some point, some or all of it will get wet.

There aren't many places to buy good replacement gear in Baja's small towns, but if you're in a bind, check out hardware stores and pharmacies. The former almost always carry kerosene lanterns; and the latter occasionally have the odd cheap tent on a shelf in the back.

Tent: Yes, some people actually kayak routes without a tent; and true enough, on perfect evenings it is wonderful to sleep beneath the stars. But those are the same people who tell harrowing stories of attacks by no-see-ums and other bugs. A tent is basic protection against such things, as well as a source of shade and shelter against the elements.

Rain is rare in most parts of Baja, but heat and wind are not. Choose a tent with large screened windows and sufficient ventilation. Any feature that adds shade, such as an extended fly, is helpful. Easy set-up and take-down are features well worth a small additional investment, since you'll be plenty tired after a day's paddling. A repair kit would include duct tape, sewing materials, and perhaps extra poles if you'll be on a very long trip.

Sleeping bag: Nights in the desert do often get cold, with temperatures as low as 40° in winter. A lightweight sleeping bag with pad, for better comfort on cobble beach campsites, is recommended.

Stove and fuel: Even the best stove has trouble during a serious, extended trip in Baja. Again, sand and salt are the culprits. Make sure you can take apart (and more importantly, put back together) any stove you buy to do regular cleaning of parts. White gas or Coleman fuel is almost always available in towns, kerosene less commonly so. Additionally, driftwood is sometimes available for fires on more remote islands and beaches.

Clothing

A supply of shorts and T-shirts for warm seasons and light pants, shirts and a jacket for cooler seasons are the basic items—to be worn over a bathing suit, of course. Year-round, you'll want to pack at least one additional warm outfit to crawl into at day's end, on cold nights, or in the event of hypothermia (this applies even at summer's peak). Beyond that, Baja poses no unique requirements. The dress code is not as formal as mainland Mexico, where shorts can invite stares, but one nice in-town outfit such as a pair of light pants, skirt or summer dress that still looks decent after scrunching is a good idea. All clothes should dry quickly.

Wetsuit or drysuit: Hypothermia is a risk wherever water temperature is less than body temperature, or 98.6°. Thus, even in the semi-tropics, you are in danger if you stay in the water long enough. Wearing normal clothing, the average adult paddler can survive 50° water for approximately 2½ to 3 hours. Therefore, in terms of emergency requirements, a wetsuit or drysuit is not necessary for most of the year in the Cortés. During winter months, or at any time of year on the Pacific, a wetsuit or drysuit is a good idea, however.

In terms of comfort, requirements are quite different. If you plan on snorkeling or spending long periods of time in the water on either coast, you may wish to bring a wetsuit or drysuit. For further clarification, see each route description for average water temperatures.

Wide-brimmed hat: A good hat with a sufficient brim to shade both face and neck should be worn at all times. A few extra bandanas that can be periodically wetted and tucked under the hat or over bare shoulders are also handy (and also double as napkins, very tiny beach towels, and much more).

Sunglasses: Essential, since the glare off both sand and water can be seriously damaging. They should be certified UVA and UVB protective and have a strap to keep them secured.

Appropriate footwear: Whether you wear the latest in surf and swimmer's footwear or an old battered pair of tennis shoes, be ready to have your feet covered for all launchings and landings. Even though the water feels soothing, there is plenty to step on: barnacles, oyster shells, sharp rocks or stingrays.

Toiletries

Shampoos, conditioners, moisturizer, sunscreen and other basic toiletries are all available in Baja, but usually at a much higher price and with much less variety. Particularly for sunscreen and lipbalm, where you want both quantity and quality (in particular, the highest SPF possible) bring your own supply.

Yel®, a brand of soap sold in Baja, suds up in saltwater better than most bars.

Tampons, birth control and contact lens solution are hard to find in camps and most towns; bring adequate supplies.

First-Aid Kit

A wilderness medicine manual (see Appendix B) can help you put together a good first-aid kit, as well as inform you on how to use it. Items specific to Baja include a snakebite kit (you probably won't use it, but just in case), Pepto-Bismol or Lomotil for diarrhea, and water-purification drops or tablets. Other essentials are: bandaids, sterile pads, tweezers, antibiotic cream, hydrogen peroxide, burn and anti-itch cream, aspirin or Tylenol. If you are allergic to bee stings, bring a bee-sting kit.

If you are on regular medication or are bringing prescription drugs with you, make sure to bring a copy of the physician's prescription and/or keep the container in which the medication came to avoid unnecessary misunderstandings with authorities. We had a little trouble when some police looked through our first-aid kit and saw the large variety of pills we'd brought for our 4-month trip. Since the police couldn't understand why any "normal" person would want to paddle hundreds of miles, they were convinced we were "on drugs."

Film and Photography

You'll kick yourself if you don't bring a camera. If you bring one, however, you'll be faced with two challenges: protection of equipment, and quick access. Reconciling the two may require some creativity.

A wide-angle lens is a must for panoramic shots. Polarizing filters help cut down sand and sea glare. If you don't want to risk your 35mm to the salt and the waves, consider one of the new disposable underwater cameras.

Color-print film is available in Baja, though usually at a slightly higher price than the U.S. Color slide and black-and-white film are more difficult to find.

Books

Anyone who doesn't share my weakness for lugging around far too many books should skip ahead. I don't travel in Baja without a wilderness medicine manual for emergencies, a basic hotel/restaurant guidebook, a AAA guide to the roads, an adventure guide for exploration farther inland, a Spanish dictionary or phrasebook, an angler's guide, fish and bird identification guides, and at least 5–10 novels to pass the hours on all those great beaches and desert isles.

Of all these, only one is really necessary for your kayak (in addition to this book, of course): the first-aid/wilderness-medicine manual. You may remember how to treat a problem in an emergency, or you may panic and forget. If you still have room after that, consider a fish or bird identification guide and a Spanish phrasebook. Both will help you experience your trip more fully. Finally, how about a journal? No one can spend time near the sea without waxing poetic.

Miscellaneous Items

Snorkel, mask and fins are a must. Spearfishing or fish trolling gear (as simple as heavy line and a few lures) will be appreciated when you tire of tacos and tamales. Solar showers sound like a good idea, but I can never find a tree on which to hang mine; a small pan of water or patient friend holding a water bag works just as well. If you have extra room, a folding camp chair will be greatly appreciated at the end of the day. A traveling chess set, pack of cards or other diversion will pass the time and make friends. Small toys and wrapped candy will make even more friends.

Food

Baja grocery stores can be very limited, particularly in small towns and camps. You will need to pack some foods, and supplement them later with Mexican staples as well as food gathered from the sea itself (fish, clams, oysters, scallops). If you have your own camping food preferences, *great*. The list that follows will help you plan by letting you know what you can count on finding almost anywhere in Baja. Bring anything that you will definitely require that is not on the list.

As for weight requirements, I don't belong to the pack-light, freeze-dried school of expedition planners. If you want to really cut down on bulk, however, keep in mind that you can dry your own fruits, veggies and even beef jerky at reasonable cost.

In preparing a food plan, include both things that can be served hot and those that can be eaten cold. Hot foods are surprisingly welcome at day's end, even in hot weather, because they seem more physically and psychologically satisfying. Hot soup or hot tea is also essential if you're wet, chilly or seriously at risk of hypothermia. Cold foods, or foods that don't need to be cooked, are good for quick breaks, lunches and—most important—for whenever your stove fails and there is no firewood to be found.

Finally, an observation about food preferences: I've noticed a strange thing that happens on long trips in Baja. After just a few weeks of kayaking, both my partner and I begin to crave foods we typically dislike, sweets in particular. Whether this is a reaction to heat or exertion, I can't be sure. But since our bodies are doing a fair share of work, we comply with any and all cravings we feel. Which brings me to the subject of calories. While kayaking 10–15 miles a day, you can eat as many of them as you'd like, and never pay the price.

Foods found in most Baja stores

White rice
Tortillas
Refried beans

Chili
Tamales
Sugar
Flour
Instant coffee
Milk
Snacks: pastries, sweets, etc.
Chocolate bars
Canned juices: pears, peach, mango, apple, etc.
Canned fruits: pear , peaches, fruit cocktail
Limited canned vegetables: corn, mixed vegetables
Tomato paste, canned tomatoes
Canned salsas and hot peppers
Canned tuna
Canned meats (e.g., Spam)
Fresh fruits and vegetables (great when available,
    but hard to find or limited in small camps and towns)
Limes
Very limited spices, garlic salt
Drink mixes: Kool-Aid, Flavor-Aid

Water and Related Equipment

To start, should you drink the water? That depends. Some people, most Americans included, have no problems with Baja's water. Others, like myself, get sick at least once each trip no matter what precautions are taken. In reality, the water in Baja is far more potable than that found on the Mexican mainland, and some would say, superior to that found just north of the border as well.

Playing it safe is easy, since *agua purificada* (purified drinking water) is available in gallon jugs at almost every mini-mart and grocery store, even in the small towns. At $1 per day, the cost of drinking bottled water for your entire trip is not unreasonable. If you get water on tap or from a questionable source, treat it with water-purification drops or tablets, boil for 30 minutes or use a portable water filter. If you crash land in some remote locale and wake up groggy with a cup being held to your lips, don't panic. Chances are the water is good. You are in more danger of getting sunstroke than any exotic disease.

To carry a sufficient water supply in your kayak, you have three options. 1) Simply stow the gallon jugs as is, if you can fit them. 2) Buy water bags (thick, square plastic bags with a spout that are carried within a fabric bag with handle) from a camping supply store. 3) Better yet, use the sturdy plastic bags that come inside boxed wine (these can double as inflatable pillows). In addition, always carry a small plastic water bottle, kept between your legs or near your seat, to encourage yourself to drink while paddling.

Final Preparations

Pre-trip paddle and rescue practice

If you haven't yet tried out your kayak, or haven't tried it loaded with gear, now is the time to do so. Contact a club or private instructor; go on a local weekend trip. If there aren't any roll or rescue clinics offered in your area, try doing what my partner and I did prior to our first trip: call the local YMCA pool and see if you can rent it for an hour or two. This certainly isn't enough time to teach yourself how to do rescues competently, but at the very least you can see what its like to fall out of your kayak and try to get back in. You might also discover that those rolls and rescues you saw illustrated in magazines and how-to books are a little more difficult than they appear. Later on, in a calm bay or estuary, you can practice more.

Final gear modifications

Now is also the time to make sure your kayak is properly adapted to your body. Seat moldings should be contoured to fit your own shape better, if necessary. The cockpit coaming should not have any sharp edges. Rudder pedals should be installed correctly so your feet can reach them with legs relaxed and bent only slightly. All seals should be watertight.

Health considerations

You should be in moderately good health before attempting a trip. Many remote areas have no medical facilities; for a serious problem, you would have to be flown back to the states. In the event of a less serious problem, there are adequate clinics and pharmacies in most towns and where noted in the text.

Vaccinations are not required for travel in Baja, but tetanus and gamma globulin shots (the latter for protection against hepatitis) are recommended. Malaria is not currently a threat on the peninsula. The best preparation for a trip is a visit to your physician; he or she can check with a travel advisory service by computer and get the latest information on what vaccinations or medications might be necessary. Often, medical advisories in effect for mainland Mexico do not apply to Baja, so specify to your physician where you're going.

Border legalities in brief

If you're going no further than Maneadero (just south of Punta Banda) and staying 72 hours or less, you don't need a tourist card. Otherwise, you'll need to obtain one from a travel club, airline, Mexican Government tourist office, consulate, embassy or immigration authority. You will need to show a passport or a certified birth certificate to obtain the card: there is no charge. A single-entry card or a multiple-entry card for 180 days is available. Cards must be validated at the border. I have never once been asked to show a tourist card while in Baja, but to avoid all hassle, make sure you're carrying one and make sure that it has been validated.

A U.S. or Canadian driver's license and proof of registration are necessary for driving in Baja. Car permits are not required unless you're planning on crossing over to the mainland. Mexican insurance is not mandatory, but highly recommended. Policies are available at the border and by mail from travel clubs and insurance brokers.

Currently, by law, boat permits are not required for kayaks in Baja. Not everyone knows this, however. On one occasion I was asked by an authority to show a permit and registration for my kayak. When I explained that neither was required, the official shrugged his shoulders and changed the subject.

If you are planning to do any fishing on your own from the beach or offshore and you are 16 years or older, you will need a license. Applications as well as information on current fees and prohibitions are available from the Mexico Department of Fisheries office, 2550 5th Ave., Suite 101, San Diego CA 92103; (619) 233 6956.

Getting There

By car: Whether you bring your own kayak or rent one along the way, you will probably transport it by car. Roof racks are available for that purpose, or you can make your own for a lot less money with one visit to the hardware store. In addition to the rack, tie down your kayak securely with ropes, both front and back, in preparation for some curvy, high-wind stretches of highway. Also, tie a red warning flag or strip of cloth to the back of your kayak.

If you've never driven in Baja, don't be too nervous. Highway 1 is fairly well maintained, and the drivers that travel it are a pretty savvy group. But do be forewarned that driving in Mexico is not like driving in the U.S. For one thing, it is more fatiguing. The roads are poorer, u-biquitous potholes and *topes* (speedbumps) demand your constant attention, there is no shoulder, and either the setting or the rising sun always seems to be in your eyes. Trips may also take a little longer, since you can't safely drive at night; cows and burros wander into the road, and those potholes are too hard to see once the sun goes down. On the positive side, it's a scenic drive, and you probably won't get lost. Most important, if you do have a breakdown, the Green Angels (Mexico's roving car-repair service) or a friendly fellow driver will give you a hand.

Travel with a road guide, such as the one offered to club members by the Automobile Club of Southern California, a branch of the American Automobile Association (AAA). Don't attempt to get to the start or finish point of the harder-to-reach routes, as described in the routes section of this book, unless you have a good off-road vehicle. For some routes, only the finish point is hard to reach; then you have the option of leaving your car at the start and doing a round-trip paddle. Other routes are planned as round-trip so there is no need to shuttle.

Once you arrive in the town or camp in which you are going to start to paddle, finding a good place to secure your car should not be too difficult. In San Felipe and La Paz, there are official car-storage establishments. Elsewhere, you can arrange to leave your car in an RV park or a hotel parking lot. In very remote places, ask a local resident or place of business for permission to leave your car parked in an approved area. Where in doubt, consult a tourism office or the local police station for advice and permission. In a town too small to have either of these, consult whoever seems to be boss. The essential component of all these suggestions is that you talk to people before leaving your car; once you make personal contact, most folks will be happy to help.

By plane: There are flights from the U.S. to Tijuana, Mexicali, San Felipe, Loreto, La Paz and Los Cabos. If you plan on renting a kayak in Loreto or Mulegé (84 miles north of Loreto) or joining a Loreto-based tour, the flight to that city can save you about 700 miles of across-border driving each way. If you're planning on joining a tour in La Paz, a flight to that city saves 922 miles.

Other options: Perhaps only in Baja do people not blink upon seeing a kayak sitting in the middle of the desert, miles from the sea. I've found myself in just that position while hitchhiking, a not altogether impractical means of transporting a kayak the length of the peninsula. By pre-arrangement, you might also strike a deal with a truck or a semi leaving Tijuana or Ensenada, particularly if it's on a return run. Or you might piggyback your kayak on the deck of a sailboat out of San Diego, particularly if you have crewing skills.

Packing Checklist (* = described in gear section)

Kayak and accessories
*Kayak with rudder, decklines, foot and knee braces
*Lifejacket (P.F.D.)
Paddle with drip rings, 1 extra paddle
Flotation bags (if necessary)
*Sprayskirt
Map case
*Drysacks for storage of all gear
Boat repair kit

Hand pump
Sponge
Drinking bottle
Extra bungee cords

Navigation and safety

*Compass
*Tide tables
*Charts/maps
*Flares, airhorn, whistle, mirror
*Yellow tow rope
Paddle float

Camping equipment

*Tent
*Sleeping bag and pad
Pillow
*Stove and fuel containers
Cook kit
Waterproof flashlight
Lantern
Towel

Food and bags to carry water

Clothing

*Basics: bathing suit, T-shirts, shorts,
light jacket, pants, one skirt or dress
*Drysuit or wetsuit
*Wide-brimmed hat
*Sunglasses with strap
*Surf or tennis shoes
Extra bandanas
Watch with alarm (or clock)

*Toiletries

*First-aid kit

*Camera and film

*Books

*Other optional items:

Snorkel and fins
Fishing equipment
Camp chair
Games, gifts
Binoculars

Chapter 3

En Route: Kayaking Baja

From dawn to dusk of a kayaking day, what is Baja really like? Before this chapter delves into the subject of specific kayaking skills and strategies, and the art of kayak touring, I thought I might conjure up a typical spring day on the Sea of Cortés.

The alarm stopped working a few days ago, but the almost imperceptible change in temperature wakes us. We unzip the sleeping bag and open the tent. The sky is pale yellow, and the Cortés, 30 feet away, as smooth as a mirror. A large, shaggy lump is crouched down in the shadows formed on one side of our tent: one of those off Mexican camp dogs that appear on the beach; friendly, unafraid. We feed him an old tortilla.

For my own breakfast, I heat some rice, add a little sugar and cinnamon. My partner, Brian, boils water for coffee. Neither of us are morning people. We yawn and scratch, and lie on the warm sand, until one of us reminds the other, "Put on suncreen! Put on your hat!" It's hard to remember in the early morning, when the sun feels so benevolent.

If we still can't wake up, we shuffle like zombies down to the water's edge and go for a cold swim. Brian goes after a tiny octopus that is clinging to the bottom of a rock. Ed Ricketts, of Steinbeck and Ricketts fame, once mentioned that he investigated every new tidepool creature by eating it. I watch my own aspiring naturalist poking something with a stick and scream when the stick gets a little too near his mouth.

It takes an hour to pack up camp. We've done it countless times, and yet we never pick up any speed. In the meantime, though, we're both completing safety checklists in our heads, figuring out what supplies should be most accessible for the day ahead, and periodically glancing at the sea and the cloudless sky to watch for the day's weather and water conditions to develop.

Before launching we look each other over, apply more sunscreen, cover our necks and shoulders with wet bandanas, and shake hands. Once on the sea, our rudders down, we finally wake up and notice our surroundings: last night's campsite to the west; a long, low point to the south; an ochre-colored island looming to the east, hovering in mirage over the opalescent morning sea. We get into the rhythm of paddling.

When I first started kayaking, I was so nervous that I periodically hyperventilated, gripped the paddle too tightly, and jumped at every far-off splash. My fingers were always numb, and my head reeled from the overstimulation of my anxious senses. Now, more relaxed, I focus on how the sea feels. Quivers vibrate faintly through the bottom of my kayak: a current or a brush against seaweed. I scan the horizon for the faintest speck which could, within a half-hour's paddle, become the sleeping form of a sea lion, reclining just below the surface with only nose and flipper tips revealed. A faint hum could be a boat or plane approaching, or surf breaking around the point a mile away; a musical lilt could be a whale. A sigh followed by clanking and rustling is inevitably Brian getting impatient and breaking open the tackle box to tow a fishing line.

Several times each hour we pull up to each other, and connect our kayaks with an outstretched paddle. We look at the map, or break out a snack. Once every hour or two we may pick up a spot on the shore and land to stretch our legs or, if we're getting hot, go for a snorkel. As the day wears on I pester Brian with questions: "What should we make for dinner? What do you look forward to eating in the next town?" We fantasize about ceviche, steak tacos, the French bakery in Santa Rosalía or fresh-grilled fish with lime and garlic. Kayaking and food to me are inseparable. I eat to get energy to paddle and I paddle to get to the mouthwatering, no-guilt cuisine of the next town or campsite.

On a really long paddle, fatigue insidiously crawls up my paddle shaft and drips into my wrists, my biceps, my shoulders, my back. At the same time, the wind begins to stir and the waves steepen. This is the part I hate, but I rarely hate it for long. Inevitably, the fatigue is wiped out by some startling event that happens at least once each day. An enormous pod of dolphins cruises by; a fish leaps over my bow. Adrenalin kicks in for the final hour as we scan the coast for a campsite.

Coming ashore at day's end always feels historic: a mixture of both the arrogant pride and nervous exuberance of the conquistador. Baja humbles the more negative aspects of that feeling, though. Baja has chewed up and spit out half a dozen conquistadors, Cortés among them. We accept the reminder.

One never knows how one will be received in a camp or a small town. Usually, where there is a cluster of Mexican fishermen gathered, we are politely tolerated and ignored. Sometimes, though, gallant young men stride down to pull our crafts above the high tideline; or children come running, curious, to pull on a bungee or simply stare. Mischievous older men will cackle, "Tiburón! Tiburón!" and cackle all the more when I reply, "No there aren't too many sharks out there anymore." Sometimes they reward my fragmented high-school Spanish with a free fish.

After the excitement of arrival passes, we drop down on the ground to feel the warmth of the sunbaked sand or the rocks. It has a definite smell, land, which one only comes to notice by taking leave of it once each day. The faint, vegetative odor of the littoral sharpens the smell, imprints it on our minds.

At the far end of the beach, I notice a heavyset gentlemen tending his panga, the name "Rosa" painted in red near its bow. Either she was a remarkable woman, this Rosa, or else someone is not terribly creative, because at least three boats in this camp bear her name. I ask the man for permission to set up a tent. He, or someone like him, always says yes, but I always ask all the same.

By dark we are well-fed, sleepy and zipped into our sleeping bags. The full moon is visible through a screened pane of our tent; spring tides are here. The term "spring" has nothing to do with the season, but is derived from the Saxon "springan": to leap. A glance outside the tent confirms how quickly the water has leaped up, well beyond the spot where we landed earlier in the day.

The only sound in camp is that of a single motor running. Through the tent door we can see a panga with two silhouettes inside, idling by the shore. A girlish laugh echoes from the bow; the popular Rosa, perhaps? And then the panga is landed, the motor is cut, and all is quiet save the whisper of water edging up the shore.

Skills and Strategies

Reading the sea

Before launching, before even taking down one's tent, the kayaker regards the sea and looks for signs. At dawn on the Cortés, you will usually see "glass" or "mirror": a nearly perfect, reflective flat sea, On the Pacific, the most gently undulating swells signal the start of a good day.

This act, a casual searching for signs that becomes habit or instinct, is sometimes called "reading the sea." On a perfect day, it's simple enough. You can hardly wait to be on that glass, that mirror; slicing a fine path before the sun has even cleared the horizon.

On a less than perfect day, or following several landings (to stretch or to snorkel) on the same day, the task is not so simple. As the day progresses and the wind stirs, the Cortés builds up waves. The Cortés waves are really wind-waves or "seas": boxy, sharp, and choppy in shape and rhythm. They are generated locally, and appear and die down with great speed.

The Pacific doesn't react so temperamentally to local conditions. Its waves are true ocean swells, caused by systems thousands of miles away. Given time, though, these swells can tower. When the swells are gentle, they appear as massive rolling hills; which, oddly enough, are sometimes easier to paddle than the smaller, choppier waves of the Cortés.

The shapes and sizes of waves, plus certain features that develop on the sea's surface, such as whitecaps or streaking foam, provide specific information about kayaking conditions. By comparing the visual appearance of the sea with descriptions in the Beaufort scale, for instance, one can even estimate wind velocity (see Appendix D for Beaufort scale). When wind velocity exceeds 20–25 mph, conditions will be too rough for all but the most experienced kayakers.

Keep in mind that the appearance of the sea will be influenced by your vantage point. Gazing seaward from your campsite, safely nestled in a cove or bay, you may not be able to see how the waves and wind are clashing just around the next point. Expect conditions to be rougher than they appear.

With experience, you will come to recognize the shapes and rhythms of both the Pacific and the Cortés, Baja's two very different bodies of water. More important, you will become proficient at seeing how a ruffled sea or bay or lagoon looks from land, gauging how it will feel in a boat, how the day's conditions will develop, and whether you should pack up or fire up a hot cup of tea instead.

Launching and landing

Reading the sea prepares you not only for deciding whether or not to paddle that day, but also for actually launching once you've decided. If the waves are lapping only gently on the shore, you can walk your kayak into the water and clamber into the cockpit as slowly and clumsily as you like. (In fact, I find I'm clumsiest when the water is calmest). When the waves are crashing, some timing is involved, and observing the sea for a bit will key you into the proper rhythm.

Watching from shore, it is possible to estimate the pattern of incoming waves. Settling quickly into your kayak between waves, you must then quickly paddle out past the line of surf before the next large wave carries you back onto shore. Sometimes you can walk your kayak out most of the way, and then jump in and paddle. Other times you must set your kayak near the waterline, wait for the water to surge and lift you up slightly and push off from there. If your partner is a more advanced kayaker and won't need any assistance, he or she can help launch you by steadying your boat and then pushing you off quickly between waves.

This description won't mean much until you've actually tried launching in a variety of conditions. To the uninitiated, the process is like trying to skip rope. You eye the rope coming around and around until you think you're timing is right and then you get in there and get moving as quickly as possible.

Landing is similar, except that you're watching from the sea and you have more responsibility in appraising the nature of the beach for which you're aiming. A beach that looks like sand from a distance may be gravel or cobble. The waves crashing on that beach are also more difficult to evaluate from the sea, since you cannot see the front part of the wave as it curls.

Optimally, choose a sheltered spot or cove in which to land. Be wary of waves that seem to plunge or dump violently, signalling an overly steep beach which will concentrate wave energy and contribute to a dangerous landing. On a more evenly sloping beach, the waves will spill more gently, without the same thundering impact.

Again, if your partner is a stronger kayaker, he or she should land first. That way you can gauge the difficulty of the landing as you watch your partner go in, and he or she can be ready to take the grabloop of your kayak and pull it above the waterline as soon as you land.

When your turn has come, position yourself just off the beach or landing spot, backpaddling if necessary to maintain your position, and take a moment to watch the patterns of the waves. Make sure that everything in your cockpit or on deck is securely fastened; you don't want to lose a camera, sunglasses or water bottle in the event of a capsize.

When you're ready, paddle quickly just after a large wave passes you and try to land just behind it. You won't have time to look back to see if another is on your tail. Paddle in a straight line, keeping perpendicular to the incoming waves. If you're not fast enough, the next wave will pick you up, turn you left or right, and dump you over. The water is probably not deep. The danger is that you might knock your head or back, get scratched up, get slammed by your own kayak, and be swept backward (while you're still trying to grab the very kayak that hit you) as the wave returns in the opposite direction.

When you do make it to shore, you must jump out and pull your kayak above the waterline before the next wave hits. You will be fighting a slight backward sucking motion that directly precedes a wave. You must move quickly, a difficult task if a long paddle leaves you stiff behind the knees. Use extra caution if the beach is composed of cobbles or boulders, or is mottled with seaweed.

If you are going to capsize or get injured at some point on your trip, it will probably be during a launching or a landing. My only Baja injury occurred at the last moment of a landing, after I was well clear of the surf zone. In a burst of machismo, I tried to pull my partner's kayak, overloaded with water, up a steep beach past the reach of waves. A quick yank, and my back snapped. I couldn't stand up straight for several days.

Simple Strokes

First, a word about the paddle. Should it be feathered (blades at right angles) or unfeathered (blades facing the same direction) This controversy reminds me of the days when schoolteachers tried to force left-handed students to write with their right hand. Obviously, you should do what is comfortable for you. You may not be able to paddle well with a feathered paddle, or you may be metaphorically ambidextrous: able to go either way. (Conveniently, many paddles are adjustable.) It may take a little time to discover which kind of paddler you are. Try both ways, and then decide.

The purpose behind a feathered paddle is the reduction of wind resistance. The blade exposed to the air, at a right angle to the blade in the water, presents less of a surface to catch the wind blowing in the kayaker's face. If you are paddling into the wind, resistance is decreased, and your speed increases. Furthermore, a feathered paddle, used properly, *can* encourage you to rotate more, and thus develop a more efficient paddlestroke. In some instances, however, feathering has a neutral or even a negative effect. If there is no wind, you don't need to feather. If the wind is gently blowing from behind, you want an unfeathered paddle to catch that wind and give you and your boat a little push.

For most cruising purposes in Baja, there really isn't a need to feather. My partner almost always does, because he prefers it. I generally do not, because when I paddle feathered for long distances I experience hand and wrist discomfort.

The forward stroke

Most of sea kayaking involves the forward stroke. It should be a simple, fluid maneuver. The first mistake most beginners make is trying to lunge at the water with their paddle, vertically stabbing at the water and losing balance and wasting energy in the process. An efficient forward stroke is much more delicate. Your goal is not to spar with the water, but to establish a rhythm of sweeping through the water gracefully on alternating sides of your craft. Aim for that rhythm first; add power later. Remember, you don't want to wear yourself ragged, because you'll probably be hoping to keep up the motion for several hours.

The key to mastering the forward stroke is the use of your entire body. Knees should be securely wedged beneath the deck. Feet should be rested on the rudder pedals. The bottom half of your body anchors you securely to the kayak. Now, as you paddle, rotate your torso. Allow your back, shoulders and waist to move freely. Your back, in particular, should do most of the work. Rather than simply punching out with alternating arms, or pushing and pulling the paddle, try moving it in a more continuous motion. (If you are in fact rotating your torso, that motion will resemble a figure-8.)

Roy Mahoff and Becky Aparicio, the kayakers who operate Baja Tropicales, liken this to the way a dolphin swims. A dolphin has no arms; it uses the continuous, rhythmic movement of its entire body to propel itself through the water.

Below deck, you may notice your legs tensing and untensing with each stroke. Your legs are carrying the momentum of the stroke while stabilizing your body within the craft. Done properly, the forward stroke works the entire body; and if you keep all muscle groups involved, you'll experience a lot less achiness on an extended trip. I used to have serious back pain and a pinched feeling behind my knees after an hour's paddle. Now that I use more of my body, I can paddle much longer without discomfort.

Having said all that, don't worry too much about book technique. It's something you can experiment with naturally while you're paddling. The above tips were explained to me time and time again by several experts, dressed up with a wide range of subtleties and metaphors. Meanwhile, I think my body disconnected from my brain and figured it out for itself. Whatever motions took some of the work away from my arms, thereby postponing fatigue, became habit.

After the forward stroke comes a whole slew of minor variations that really aren't much more difficult. The backward stroke is the reverse of the above, which logically moves you backward. The draw stroke pulls your boat toward your paddle. The sculling draw stroke, a series of small figure-8's done on one side of your kayak, has the same effect while enhancing stability. The sweep stroke, a widely arcing stroke, turns your boat in the direction opposite that in which you're sweeping, particularly when executed just as you're cresting a wave. High and low braces provide quick recovery, restoring your balance when you're upset by a wave or on the verge of tipping during a less-than-perfect landing. Study illustrated examples of these moves and practice in calm to moderate conditions.

Wind

"Febrero loco, Marzo poco más": "Crazy February, March a little more of the same." I don't believe I've ever read a boating article about winter conditions in Baja that didn't mention this Mexican saying. The funny thing is, I've never actually heard a *Mexican* say it. Usually, when a northerly has been howling fiercely for a few days, the only commentary I've heard a Mexican make is simply, "Ay, el viento": "Ay, the wind." Hearing this, I usually cringe and develop a pained, exasperated look on my face, which inevitably causes the Mexican to laugh.

The wind in Baja is rarely avoidable, but usually predictable. Daily and seasonal patterns are fairly consistent, give or take the odd 3–5 day howler that keeps everyone on land.

Daily patterns

Dawn and dusk are generally tranquil times. The really smart kay-aker—and this doesn't include myself—gets most of his or her miles done before noon or so. After this time, the wind usually increases in strength and prompts kayakers to head to shore to set up camp and relax for the rest of the day. (Often, the afternoon wind is from the land, making it difficult to get to shore. For this reason, plan on stopping for the day before you reach the point of exhaustion.)

Exceptions to this rule are numerous. If northerlies have been blow-ing all night, the sea may not have time to flatten out by morning. In the La Paz area, the legendary *coromuel* wind starts blowing in the evening, and it may contribute to a rumpled, if not tempestuous, dawn sea. In the Magdalena Bay area on the Pacific, winds seem to get whipped up at all times of day and night. Though I'm sure some legend or adage has been coined in honor of the gusts that blow over the dunes and force campers to eat sand, I haven't heard it yet.

Daily wind patterns are influenced by the flow of air over the mountainous spine of the peninsula; this is in turn influenced by the change in temperature as air is warmed and cooled each day. Storm sys-tems also play a role, of course. Additionally, Mexicans believe that wind patterns are related to lunar cycles. To combine all these variables, meteorological expertise is helpful; or, more simply, one could just ask a local fisherman for his hunch.

Seasonal patterns

Winds in the Pacific are usually from the northwest. Winter storm sys-tems may disrupt this pattern, bringing wind from the southwest or southeast.

Winds on the Cortés blow from the northwest from November to May. The strongest of these, the winter northerlies, are felt from Decem-ber to March. These winds can build up with great speed, surprising a kayaker in the middle of a long crossing; use extreme caution whenever you are more than one mile offshore. The rest of the year, winds are more variable. During *chubasco* (tropical stormy season, from late sum-mer to early fall, strong winds can blow from the southwest to south-east. Short, fierce spells of westerly wind can funnel down the mountains at any time.

Coping

"When is this damn wind going to go away?" I finally demanded on the second or third day of my last visit to Bahía de Los Ángeles, as a persistent spell of wind shook the town. A member of the Díaz clan heard my impatient question. "Go away?" he retorted, "That wind *lives* here." Good to remember, I guess. If you're going to get along with the elements, the best strategy is simple patience. As long as you stay flexible, and bring plenty of food and water, you should be able to wait out the worst spells of bad wind or weather, and enjoy the gentler spells with the tact and appreciativeness of a proper guest.

Tides and Tidal Currents

The ceaseless actions of the tides ensure that few parts of the Baja coast ever look the same way twice in a day. You may go to sleep on a broad, fine tawny-colored beach, only to awake to an immense field of ugly, black, pock-marked boulders stretching beyond that sandy zone.

With the rockier foreshore revealed, you may find yourself facing a precarious portage and a more difficult launch, unless you wait for the high tide to return. Depending on the current phase of the lunar cycle, the high tides of the nights to come may immerse your perfect campsite completely. Once you do commence paddling, you may find that the tides create strong currents through narrow passages. In other words, the tides will affect your activities both on land and at sea, and inevitably, you will have to take their fluctuations into consideration.

The tides are produced by the combined forces of the earth, sun and moon. The sun and the moon exert gravitational pull on the waters of the earth, creating slight bulges. As the earth rotates, these bulges move, bringing rising and falling tides to coasts around the world. When the sun and moon are lined up, either on the same side or on opposite sides of the earth, they act together, creating tides with a larger differential: higher highs, lower lows. This happens during the full and new moons, causing "spring tides." When the sun and the moon are at right angles, they cancel each other out somewhat. This happens during the first and last quarters of each lunar cycle, creating tides that are not as significant: "neap tides."

The tides have such a dramatic effect on the northern Cortés in particular because of the gulf's long, narrow shape. In completing a daily cycle, two highs and two lows each tidal day, the water must race a mighty distance at an impressive speed. In the midriffs in particular, that belt of islands near the middle of the Sea of Cortés, the movement of water creates strong tidal currents and whirlpools. Nutrients are drawn up from the cool depths in this process, creating a lively feeding ground which benefits every member of the food chain, from zooplankton to marine mammals.

Because the tidal day is 24 hours and 50 minutes long, high and low tides come successively later each day. To know when the tide will be high, and how high it will be in a given place, the kayaker should consult a tide table. Tide tables give times and tide heights for widely spaced tidal stations. To read the chart, simply look for the station that is closest to your present position.

When the tide is rising, it is called a flood tide. When the tide is falling, it is called an ebb tide. The brief time between these is called slack water; there is little movement and less tidal current at this time, providing the optimum period for risky crossings or passage between islands. For a more in-depth look at this subject, consult David Burch's *Fundamentals of Kayak Navigation*.

There are some places where a tide table is not entirely necessary. In Bahía Concepción, for example, the tides don't fluctuate greatly. Elsewhere, without a tide table, you may run into trouble. The best way to estimate tides without a table is simply to look for the line of debris and seaweed on a beach; that is the most recent high tide. If the moon is moving toward a full or a new phase, the next high tide (or the one following) will be higher yet. If the moon is moving toward a quarter phase, the next high tide (or the one following) will be a little lower.

Particularly when you are in doubt, tie your kayak to something stable to prevent it from floating away, and be prepared to wake to a soggy tent floor. If you're truly in a confused panic, set your alarm clock to wake you up every few hours to check on the approach of the waterline. It is not a restful way to pass a night, but it will certainly prompt a new appreciation for the mysterious cycles of the earth, sun, moon and seas.

Final Cautions: Waves And Currents

Mention of waves has already been made in the sections on reading the sea and launching and landing. Additionally, there are some specific areas and situations where waves as well as currents may require a kayaker's careful attention.

Waves are often reflected off of sheer cliffs, headlands, and structures such as piers. These reflected waves may meet incoming waves and create choppy, confused seas. Currents are also often strong around headlands.

When winds and currents are going in opposite directions, seas will be more rough. Glassy ribbons on a more roughly textured sea guide the kayaker to those areas where wind and current are moving in the same direction.

Islands pose unique challenges. For one thing, waves tend to refract around the sides of an island and set up interference patterns, especially where two or more islands are in a cluster. And currents tend to be strong between two islands or an island and the mainland, or in fact anywhere that rushing water must pass through a constricted space.

Waves or swells that are striking the front of your craft may seem problematic, but they are actually fairly easy to paddle over. When they strike the side of your craft, however, you may have to brace or lean into the waves to prevent a capsize. A little wave or swell action from behind may give you a free ride, but when following seas gain momentum they may impair your control by causing your kayak to swing slightly left or right as you "surf" down the wave.

Navigation

Anyone serious about learning the art and science of navigation should read David Burch's *Fundamentals of Kayak Navigation*. Though most of its examples are taken from the Pacific Northwest, it is a comprehensive and well-illustrated manual on just about every aspect of navigation. Having said that, let me briefly review some of the aspects of navigating in Baja that may be different from other popular sea-kayaking areas.

Two of the most typical navigational challenges, fog and heavy traffic, are generally absent in Baja. On the Pacific, woollen skies are common; but on the Cortés, visibility is almost always assured. As for boat traffic, it is usually so spread out or scarce as to be insignificant except within one or two small harbor mouths. Also different in Baja is the extent of navigational aids. Particularly in the Sea of Cortés, buoys and beacons and even lighthouses are not very common or reliable (the latter may be present, but out of operation).

Instead, Baja has some navigational challenges and peculiarities of its own. In some areas, a lack of landmarks makes judging one's position difficult. This is particularly true in flat areas with monotonous topographical features, such as the long dune stretches south of San Felipe, and the winding mangrove channels of the Pacific's Magdalena lagoons. The lack of development or population doesn't help. On a coast that has no houses, cars or people to provide visual perspective, it is often difficult to judge one's distance offshore until one tries paddling back to land. Perhaps most notoriously, mirages simply fool the eye. A point that appears close may be very far away; an island that appears far may be close.

Where there are few coastal landmarks or offshore islands, I usually turn my compass toward inland mountain peaks. For this reason, I recommend topographical maps over nautical charts, since they cover inland mountain ranges and feature more extensive shoreline detail. When navigating with map and compass, don't forget to adjust for the variation (known as "declination" on land) between magnetic and true north. Variation in Baja ranges from 14° east in the north to 10° east in the south. For more information on maps and charts, see Chapter 2.

If you are truly lost, you will probably try to consult the first fellow boater or fisherman you see to find out the location of the closest town or camp. Fisherman and fellow boaters are great sources of information on water availability, fishing conditions, weather, etc., but I can't conclude this section without adding a few warnings and a recommendation that you be critical in evaluating all information you receive.

When it comes to estimating distances, few coastal travelers speak the same language as the kayaker. To motorized boaters who travel three times faster than you, an error of 3–5 miles may not seem like much. Be particularly wary of gamefishermen clutching cans of beer who swear that a resort is "just a few minutes down that way." That "few minutes" may take a kayaker half a day, and if you're anxious or ailing, that half a day will seem like an eternity.

More subtle misunderstandings may occur if you ask a local fisherman for specific information. On one occasion when my partner and I were dangerously low on water and supplies, a fisherman was kind enough to give us a lift by panga in the direction of the next town. Dropping us off in the middle of nowhere, he pointed south and assured us that the town was "30 kilometers south," the absolute maximum we could paddle with the supplies that remained.

I checked my map and compass. The position of a nearby island didn't seem right. "30 kilometers south? Are you sure you don't mean 30 *miles* south?" I asked.

The fisherman looked flustered, and started gunning his motor. "Kilometers, miles . . . whatever" he grumbled under his breath, "I'm in a hurry." As it turned out, we were not 30 kilometers, even 30 miles, but 40 miles away from the next town.

Rescues

An Eskimo roll is the most efficient and glamorous way to resume paddling after a capsize, but many sea kayakers don't know how to do one. Even among those who can execute a roll in still conditions with an unloaded kayak, only a minority can manage the same feat in rough conditions with a fully loaded craft.

In a worst-case scenario, a paddler may respond to capsizing by swimming to shore. Hopefully, though, you will be able to get back into your kayak, bail out excess water, and resume paddling. To that end, there are a great number of rescue techniques which can be employed. All of them should be practiced in advance of an actual emergency.

My own compliance with that fine advice is pretty spotty. I used to reason that I would be able to perform a self-rescue if and when the need arose. Like a feeble octogenarian who is suddenly imbued with strength enough to lift cars or steel beams during a time of crisis, I assumed I'd become suddenly more graceful and competent in the event of a capsize. Not so. During an emergency, the average person becomes only more muddle-headed and clumsy. Unless a rescue is practiced in advance, it won't be successful.

Crawling back into your kayak, particularly when it's destabilized by water, is tricky—a little like log-rolling. One way to make it easier is to attach a paddle float, an inflatable or foam sleeve, to the end of your paddle. With one end of the paddle secured under a deckline and the other end buoyed by the paddle float, the paddle itself becomes an outrigger stabilizing your craft and enabling you to climb back inside. If you bring a paddle float, make sure it is accessible: not packed away in a drysack somewhere deep inside your boat.

With assistance from one or more kayakers, other rescues are possible. A partner or partners can raft up by extending paddles across their cockpits and, with the swamped boat in the middle, providing enough stability for the capsized kayaker to crawl back in and pump out. The H-I Rescue, similar to this, involves lifting the swamped boat perpendicularly over the other two kayaks to empty the water (picture the swamped kayak as the crossbar in the letter "H") and then stabilizing it between the two kayaks to allow for re-entry. The T-Rescue involves positioning the swapped boat perpendicular to one other kayak, lifting it up over the bow and emptying the water, pulling the kayak back into a parallel position and holding it steady for re-entry.

Emergencies: Assistance from Third Parties

What if you have an injury? What if you run out of water? Even in the remote coastal regions of Baja, one can usually hope to see other humans at least once every few days. Small, private planes often pass over. More commonly, fishing boats ply the coast. Mexican pangas are seen on both the Cortés and the Pacific. In the southern Cortés, a good number of yachts also pass within signalling distance of the coast. American dunebuggies occasionally zip by on the beaches of the northern Cortés.

Don't be too nervous or ashamed to signal any of these potential rescuers. Even if you don't speak Spanish, Mexican fishermen may be very helpful in providing water or a lift to the nearest camp or town. The code of ethics both on the sea and in the desert is to help those in need; it's simply too inhospitable a place for humans to survive there in any other fashion.

One of the most dangerous ways to seek assistance is to strike off into the desert after an aborted kayak trip. Out of simple frustration or dire distress, several individuals and groups have tried this. Where the highway runs close to the shore, this is logical. But where 5, 10 or 20 miles of blazing hot desert stand between the sea and the closest road, this is foolhardy. Certainly don't wander into the desert without knowledge of the area, and/or a map and compass; and, when at all possible, stay in the shade and shelter of a campsite while trying to signal a passing boat instead.

The Art of Touring: Planning, Packing and Pacing

You don't want to be tied to a schedule, but you should have a general idea of how far you intend to paddle and where you hope to arrive at the end of each day. This book has stressed several times that delays and distractions will probably change those plans, but at least they'll give you a starting point.

Armed with maps, the routes section of this book, and any local information you've gleaned during your stay, you can look for good potential campsites within your daily mileage capabilities, places to get water or supplies if you need them, and good snorkeling, hiking or shade areas en route to provide breaks from kayaking.

Keep in mind that early morning is the best time to paddle. Rise with plenty of time to pack up camp; it may take more time than you think to cram all that gear back into your kayak.

Make sure anything you'll need during the day's paddle will be accessible, either stashed in your map case, tucked under your decklines within arm's reach of the cockpit, or behind your seat. Items to keep close at hand include: navigational, signalling and self-rescue devices; hand-pump and sponge; sunscreen, lip-balm, sunglasses and drinking water; camera and fishing gear if you intend to use them. If you don't want to eat breakfast, pack something substantial in your map case to eat later. In packing away the bulk of your remaining gear, stow the heaviest stuff toward the middle and bottom of your craft for greatest stability, with smaller and lighter items wedged into the kayak's ends.

Hydrate yourself religiously during each day's paddle, and keep an eye on fellow group members to make sure they do the same. Water may taste unappealing once it's warm, or if purification tablets have been added. I usually detest sweet drink mixes; but while kayaking, particularly in a hot climate, they are very helpful. Be careful about dehydration and sunstroke, since you may not know you're in danger until it's too late. You may not even feel thirsty or terribly hot; you may just get cranky, irrational or giddy.

Don't plan for any major challenges late in the day, including crossing to an island, since wind and/or heat may pose difficulties. Don't paddle past a good beach or cove for camping if you're tired or it's late in the afternoon; particularly if the next one is not for several miles. Allow yourself plenty of time to set up camp and lay out anything that has got damp while a few hours of sunlight remain.

Camping in Mexico: Law, Custom and Courtesy

Camping in Mexico is very different than in the U.S. Paddling New England or the Pacific Northwest, you may have to call or write landowners in advance and limit your stays to official campsites. In Mexico, on the other hand, the beach belongs to the people.

Camping doesn't have the same social stigma here as elsewhere. Respectable middle-class families often set up camps in droves, particularly in places like San Felipe and Ensenada. If a Mexican and all his possessions are occupying a small blanket on the beach, he is not a vagrant, he is exercising his constitutional right! So say both law and custom. But how do they apply to you, the visitor?

For the most part, particularly in remote areas, you simply pull up to a beach or cove and unpack. There are many stretches where you will not see another soul. If other campers or kayakers are there, you can keep going to find your own spot or you can stay and share the space amiably.

If the beach is commandeered by a large hotel or resort, you can often still camp there. Technically, the waterfront is still public domain. For all practical purposes, resort owners don't seem to mind the intrusion of someone quietly pulling up by sea as much as someone barreling through in a dunebuggy or 4-wheel-drive truck.

On a beach that has become touristy or well-known for camping, someone will sometimes come around to collect a fee. This is understandable where there are some amenities, like palapas, showers or pit toilets. Where there are no amenities, the legal issue of charging for camping is more ambiguous. If the fee is unreasonable you can try to bargain it down a bit, or you may prefer to simply pack up and head a little farther down the coast.

Where the fee is very small, I prefer to pay it. If an older Mexican man, for instance, comes to collect his $2, I pay and use the time as an opportunity to introduce myself, ask questions, and explain my trip. Later, then, if I need to go into town or leave my kayak unattended, I can ask him to keep an eye on my possessions.

In a nontouristy locale such as a small, remote Mexican fishing camp, I ask permission before I set up a tent. I don't offer to pay, but I do introduce myself to whoever seems to be in charge. Later, children will occasionally visit my tent and act as go-betweens, offering water or accepting small gifts.

Camping: Common-Sense and Conservation

Legal and customary issues aside, there are several important points to consider in choosing a campsite. Don't set up near mangroves, lagoons or brushy areas where *jejenes* (no-see-ums) and other bugs, snakes and nasties lurk. Also beware of cacti, particularly the jumping cholla, whose spiny nubs break off and adhere like painful velcro to your shoes and bottom. Make sure your camp is well above the high-tide line; some nice beaches are off-limits to camping because they become fully submerged during high tide.

Camping on islands requires special care and self-restraint. Since 1978, all hunting and foraging has been prohibited on islands. Even stopping or setting up camp on some islands is a questionable if not illegal activity, since humans can disrupt roosting and nesting birds and breeding sea lions. At certain times of the year, even one brief visit by a human can panic birds and cause them to abandon their nesting sites.

The routes section in this book attempts to point out those particularly sensitive locations, but in reality all islands are ecologically vulnerable. Limit your hiking on them; be careful about disturbing birds and wildlife. If you do camp, do so in areas already in use for that purpose. If a campsite smells or is fly-ridden, it is most definitely being used by masses of birds; all the more reason to leave the area and find a less disruptive place for your tent. If you are really concerned about not doing damage, don't camp on the smaller islands at all. Cruise the shore, observe from a distance, and then paddle back to the mainland to camp for the night.

When you do set up camp, tie your kayak to something stable or anchor it with a long line to prevent it from floating away. Since small foraging animals can be a problem, secure your food bags inside your kayak and close down the hatches, or bring your food bags inside your tent with you.

On the subject of using driftwood to build fires, most kayakers are divided. In remote places, when I come across old crates and sticks, I do build a fire, but some recent articles have suggested that wood is scarce and should be left to local fishermen. When you leave a site, pack out all your garbage. Be particularly conscientious about removing plastics and fishing line, which will not degrade.

These last points bring me to some thoughts about the environment and Baja. Many visitors are disturbed by the amount of garbage they see. Which is worse, however: to bury nontoxic garbage in a landfill, where it will degrade more slowly, or to leave it to the salt, wind, desert air and vultures? Mexicans tend to do the latter. Unfortunately, neither hiding garbage in landfills nor leaving it out in the open are optimal waste management strategies. As a visitor, probably the best thing you can do is reduce and re-use as much as possible. Luckily, kayakers don't tend to have much room for the excess junk that makes garbage in the first place, but we do have enough room to stow our empty cans and bottles, as well as any garbage we encounter along the way. Maybe we can set a good example.

As Mexico becomes more concerned about conservation, and as *ejido* (public land) laws change, camping regulations both on islands and on the peninsula may become more stringent. Try to keep abreast of any changes by asking local residents or fellow campers and kayaker.

Natural Perils

Most real perils you will face will be cumulative (dehydration, overexposure to sun) or specific to kayaking (handling waves, landings). Those basic safety concerns and on-the-sea skills and strategies are discussed elsewhere in this chapter. What worries most people in planning a trip to the desert or the coast are more specific and exotic perils, usually involving some member of the animal kingdom. Since most of these are likely to affect you while you're camping or swimming, rather than paddling, I've chosen to deal with them in this section.

I've always had bad luck with anything that bites or stings. I've been attacked by a goat, had my hand chomped by a burro, and even had a very small fish take a nip out of my knee (in a freshwater lake, not in Baja). Witnesses will attest to these facts. Perhaps it is something in my pheromones. In any case, a little trepidation might be understandable whenever I venture far from home. Nonetheless, I have never had any serious problems in Baja. I'll list the potential threats, but I don't think they're much cause for concern.

Rattlesnakes, scorpions and spiders (specifically, black widows) are best avoided by shaking out your shoes, camping in a cleared area, and abstaining from sticking your hand into anything (including your kayak) without looking. Palapas, though delightful for shade, also provide hiding places for crawling things. Scrutinize or stay clear of corners and dark places. Snakebites are rare, but you probably should carry a snakebite kit anyway. Scorpions are more common, but not as common or as dangerous as most people think. Graham Mackintosh, author of *Into A Desert Place*, walked 3000 miles in Baja and got stung only twice. Few scorpion stings are fatal, except where the victim is a small child or has a heart condition. Usually there is some numbness and pain for a few days. Treatment involves staying calm and still, cooling the area with ice when possible, sucking large quantities of limes and applying lime juice or crushed garlic to the sting.

Stingrays can plant their barb in the back of your heel or ankle if you have the misfortune of stepping on one. Give them warning by shuffling your feet in sandy areas; generally, they'll scoot away. If you do get stung, soak the wounded foot in water as hot as you can tolerate. Some fish, such as the scorpionfish are also dangerous to step on; all the more reason to wear thick-soled shoes and watch where you step.

Bees and wasps seem to be attracted by bright colors. On one particularly remote beach, our kayaks were covered by them. They didn't bother us until I accidentally killed one, and then all hell broke loose. The bees behaved in an unusually aggressive manner. The tent, hastily half-erected, provided protection until dusk, when both bees and wasps went away. This happened only once, but be forewarned if you have an allergic reaction to stings.

Jellyfish, or *agua mala*, can cause a prickly or stinging sensation if you encounter them. Urine neutralizes the poison. I've never had a serious enough encounter to require any response or treatment besides simply getting out of the water.

Sharks have always been my number-one fear anytime I get near the sea. As a member of the "Jaws" generation, I personally blame Peter Benchley for my paranoia. In reality, I now sadly realize that there isn't much to fear. Most sharks are harmless, and most have been fished out of the Sea of Cortés. Hammerheads congregate in a few areas, such as the Marisla Seamount, where scuba divers and documentarians seek them out; but in most areas, sharks are scarce. There isn't much sense in panicking over every fin spotted in the water; more often than not, you are seeing a sea lion, a ray or a dolphin.

Natural Pleasures

Wildlife watching

From the kayak or the campsite, Baja is a great place to watch animals. Over 20 species of cetaceans populate Baja's waters. Bottlenose and common dolphins are frequent companions on many kayak trips, and few experiences equal the sighting of a whale: blue, fin, gray, Bryde's, Sei, Minke and humpbacks all visit or populate local waters. The vaquita, a porpoise on the verge of extinction (only 200 remain) is occasionally spotted in the northern gulf, usually within 25 miles of San Felipe; it is one of the rarest cetaceans in the world.

Land mammals include creatures you may never glimpse, such as mountain lions and bobcats, and ones that may get curious enough to pay a visit to your tent: ring-tailed cats, badgers and chipmunks, to name a few. The howl of the coyote pierces the desert night on many evenings.

Birdwatchers have their heyday in Baja, since over 400 species live in or pay visits to the peninsula and its surrounding islands and waters. Even if you're ornithologically illiterate, you'll probably come to recognize your most ubiquitous avian escorts: pelicans, cormorants, frigatebirds, boobies and gulls.

In addition to the animals mentioned above, there are many endemic species, such as the black jackrabbit and fish-eating bat. In addition to fauna, there is a wealth of flora, including more species of cacti than anywhere else in the world. Of interest to those prepared for underwater adventures, there are the Pacific manta and the enormous whale shark, both of which have been known to let divers grab on for a ride.

On all these subjects, entire volumes have been written. Books worth reading include *The Baja Adventure Book* by Walt Peterson, which includes a great overview of Baja's "natural wonders" including many anecdotes about personal encounters with wildlife, both on land and at sea. *The Gray Whale*, edited by Mary Lou Jones, Steven L. Swartz and Stephen Leatherwood, explains the history and ecology of that animal, good background reading if you're making your own migration to any of the Pacific lagoons where the gray whale calves and breeds. *Island Biogeography in the Sea of Cortez*, edited by Ted J. Case and Martin L. Cody, is a scholarly volume of interest to serious wildlife watchers, particularly those interested in the distribution of endemic species.

For the tidepool explorer, there is really only one book. *The Log From the Sea of Cortez* by John Steinbeck and Ed Ricketts inspired several generations of Baja aficionados with its odd combination of tidepool ecology, stream-of-consciousness philosophy and humorous rantings and ravings about all the things that can go wrong during a boating adventure.

Fishing

Before kayakers ever considered visiting Baja's coastal warm waters, the fishermen came. Angler-oriented hotels were built. Celebrities like Bing Crosby flew down to battle with prize sailfish. After the highway was completed and sideroads were improved, even more people visited Baja in hopes of reeling in any of the over 800 species of fish that inhabit area waters.

For the kayaker, fishing is a great diversion and a way to supplement one's diet. Trolling from one's cockpit can be surprisingly successful. Before my partner and I ever tried it, we worried about catching something too big and having our boats capsize in the ensuing struggle. That hasn't happened yet. If something big strikes, which is rare, we lose a lure. Smaller fish, even ones that put up an admirable fight don't threaten the stability of our kayaks.

To troll from a kayak cockpit, use 60-pound test line or above. Lighter line will almost always snap, even with small fish. A length of rope should be attached to one end of the line for ease of handling in pulling in the line; the very end of this rope remains coiled in the paddler's lap. Silver spoons are good all-purpose lures to use.

The slow, steady movement of the kayak keeps the line and the rope trailing nicely behind the kayak, although occasionally they will get stuck on weeds or rocks. Occasional tugging to check for fish or weeds can be done between stretches of paddling when water conditions are calm. That's the basic system. I'm sure kayakers have worked

out countless variations, using spools and bungees and more sophisticated lures.

Trolling from a kayak, my partner has caught croaker, corvina,
roosterfish, triggerfish, barracuda, yellowtail and several kinds of bass,
plus the odd needlefish, pufferfish and porcupinefish. I haven't had as
much success, but I always appreciate his efforts after several nights of
macaroni and cheese.

Snorkeling

Fin, mask and snorkel come in handy anytime you land to take a break
from kayaking. Islands and rocky beaches in the lower Cortés are the
best spots. The drabbest cobble beaches tend to feature the most remarkable offshore snorkeling. I'm always astonished by the explosion
of life and color that is visible in water only a few feet deep, once you
don a mask.

With an open-top kayak, you don't have to land each time you
want to snorkel. With a kayak leash tied to your wrist, you can tow your
kayak along with you as you watch fish or seek out clams for dinner.

In exceptional spots like the southern end of Isla Carmen, the mask,
fins and snorkel aren't even necessary. Gazing down from your cockpit
you will see sergeant majors and parrotfish, wrasses and slim, silver
cornetfish just under the surface.

Other pursuits

Kayaking can be paired well with countless other land and sea pursuits:
exploring sea caves, searching for shipwreck sites, or hiking remote terrain accessible only by boat. For ideas, inspiration and geographical information, read Walt Peterson's *The Baja Adventure Book*. Stargazing is
also excellent in Baja, so you may want to pack a star chart for the trip.
On a remote beach, far from city lights, in a cloudless desert clime, the
stars seem to shine more brightly here than almost anywhere else on the
continent.

Staying Healthy

"No . . . " you groan, "Not more advice about water!" Well, yes; drinking up to a gallon of purified water a day is your best preventive health
strategy. Getting enough rest, seeking out shade whenever possible,
keeping your head covered and avoiding overexertion are also essential. In addition to those things, here are a few tips for staying healthy en
route.

Get out of the sun before you see the burn; it won't show up until
later. One day's burn can ruin your plans for a week.

Be alert for headaches, dizziness, a weak pulse or cold, clammy
skin. These are some of the first signs of heat exhaustion. Treat by reclining in the shade, fanning and wetting skin and drinking plenty of water.

Be alert for symptoms of sunstroke; if condition worsens, seek medical help if possible.

Take time off from paddling if you start developing wrist pain. You may be able to correct your stroke and lessen the pain somewhat, but usually it just keeps building until you demobilize it for a few days.

Garlic and lime juice are supposed to kill bacteria and parasites. Keep them on hand for fish marinades, clambakes, and rice dishes, as well as random medicinal needs.

If you do get traveller's diarrhea, you can either take one of the classic medicines, such as Lomotil, or you can wait it out. The latter may actually be the healthier strategy and is a lot easier on your system. Avoid caffeine and spices, get plenty of water and rest. It will usually pass within 3 days. You may find this a good time to store your kayak temporarily (ask someone to watch it for you), check into a hotel with a comfy bed and clean bathroom, and catch up on your postcards home.

In Town

At trip's end, or at regular intervals on a long trip, you will arrive in small towns and cities ready to sample civilization's finest offerings. After a week on the seas, communities of 10,000 souls seem like immense, lively metropolises. You may be dazzled by the offerings of food and shelter and run wildly into the heart of town, leaving your poor kayak abandoned on the beach.

This is what I did. Once. My kayak, considered abandoned by the authorities, was quickly confiscated. With a little finagling, I got it back, and I learned my lesson. On recounting this story, many friends have lambasted me. How could I be so careless? How could I be so stupid? My excuses: mild sunstroke, town-induced euphoria, and an upset stomach in desperate search of a bathroom. Also, something about Baja's laid-back atmosphere contributes to a naivete that would be instantly ridiculed and exploited north of the border. I know I certainly wouldn't have done something so dumb back home.

Crime in small towns and cities is rarely a problem, but don't let your guard completely down. When you foray into more urban areas, ask someone (local resident, lighthouse keeper, harbor master, restaurant owner) to keep an eye on your kayak for you.

To explore developed areas, carry a small guide to area hotels and restaurants. If you're looking for telephones or full-service post office, be forewarned that if a town is not on Highway 1 or a major sideroad, it may not have such modern amenities. This includes most of the northern Cortés south of San Felipe."

How to Use the Routes

The route descriptions that follow are suggestions only. They are intended to help you plan where you'd like to go, rather than to be strict itineraries once you've started paddling. Mileage is given in statute miles, not nautical miles. *Maps are intended for planning purposes only, not for navigation.* Please keep in mind that many islands and locations have more than one name; I have tried to give both the English and Spanish names where possible, as well as the most common alternate names.

Many of the places named in the text and on the maps are "camps" (*campos* in Spanish). These are small communities, sometimes temporary or seasonal. American vacation or retirement camps are typically composed of 10–70 RVs, palapa or stone huts, or houses. Mexican fishing camps are typically composed of a small number of shacks, usually constructed of plywood, or palapa huts. While camps seldom have accommodations or services for the traveler, they may be able to provide water or emergency assistance, and a few have airstrips or roads connecting up with major roads or highways farther inland.

Some routes are described as round-trip, while others start and finish at points far apart. If you plan on kayaking the latter kind, you will have to plan your transportation accordingly. Unless you are in a group that arranges to leave a vehicle at each end of a route, or you have somebody to pick you up at the end, you will probably have to find a way to get yourself, with or without your kayak, back to the starting point where you have left your vehicle. Hitchhiking is often an option, particularly where mentioned in the text. If you hitchhike without your kayak, you'll have to make a final trip back to the finish point to pick up your kayak. (The same is true if you take a bus or a taxi.) If you hitchhike with your kayak (possible in some cases if you bring lots of rope and find a willing driver) you cut out one part of the shuttle.

In Baja, both the natural environment and the increasing pace of development contribute to an ever-changing coastline. Daily or seasonal conditions may also change the appearance and nature of many locations. Aim to supplement this guidebook with local information and advice, and, most important, a healthy dose of common sense. Although the author and the publisher cannot be responsible for errors, the author welcomes any corrections, comments, suggestions or anecdotes that might be helpful for future editions.

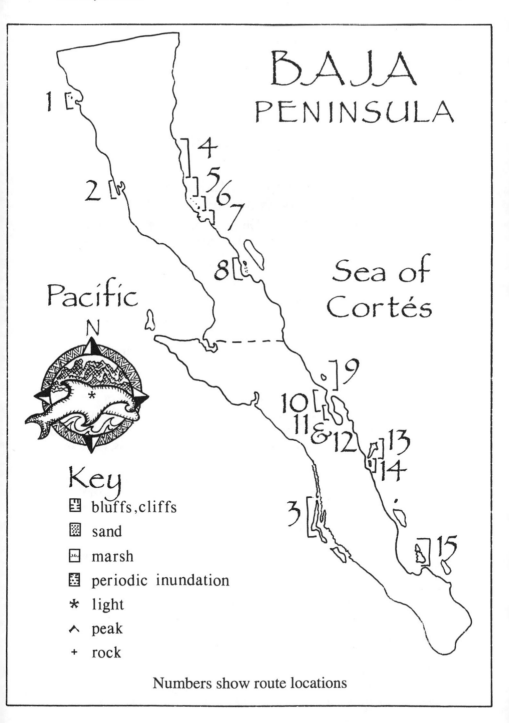

BAJA
PENINSULA

1

4
5
6
7

2

8

Pacific

Sea of
Cortés

N

9

10
11 & 12
13
14

Key
3

bluffs, cliffs

sand

marsh

periodic inundation

* light

∧ peak

+ rock

15

Numbers show route locations

Chapter 4

The Baja Pacific

ROUTE 1   Border Hop: Punta Banda and Las Islas de Todos Santos

Trip Summary: An 18.5-mile trip along the northern shore of a rugged peninsula just south of Ensenada, out to two small islands via a 4-mile crossing, and back to the southern shore of the peninsula for a look at La Bufadora, a sea-cave blowhole.

Trip Length: 2–3 days.

Charts: MEX Topo H11 B1, H11 B22 at 1:50,000; U.S. Nautical 21021

Getting There: From the border city of Tijuana take Highway 1-D (the tollroad) or Old Highway 1 to Ensenada. Continue on Highway 1 for 10 miles toward Maneadero. Just north of Maneadero, Highway 1 junctions with Highway 23, a paved road to Punta Banda. Highway 23 proceeds west for 7–8 miles to base camps of La Jolla and Villarino (signed).

Total trip time from the border is about 2½ hours; more on the weekend. Be *extra* cautious about *topes* (road bumps) along the way, especially just south of Ensenada. Remember that with kayaks and camping gear weighing down your car, *topes* can be more jostling than they appear.

Climate & Conditions: The area surrounding Ensenada has a climate more similar to San Diego than to the rest of Baja. Winter temperatures in the 40–50°s, summer temperatures 70–80°s. The area receives about 10 inches of rainfall per year, mostly between December and March. Occasional fog is common year-round.

Water surface temperature ranges from 59° in January to 66° in July.

Wind is predominantly from the northwest at 5–6 knots, with slightly stronger winds reported in the winter.

Like most routes in the Pacific, this route is best done in summer. The climate is at its most comfortable while the rest of Baja simmers.

When I looked at the maps, I was skeptical. Punta Banda looked too close to Ensenada, too close to the border in general, to be untouched by that congested region's pollution, industry, tourism and population overflow. I couldn't imagine much wildlife would still thrive there. Nor, given the urban nature of northern Baja, did I expect much in the way of scenery or solitude.

Nonetheless, I planned a trip. And happily, my skepticism was unfounded. Punta Banda's proximity to the border (only 85 miles or 2½ hours) and accessibility (no tourist card required) haven't destroyed its charm. Although there is some shipping traffic in nearby Ensenada, relatively few boats prowl around the point itself. (Abundant offshore rocks make the waters dangerous for many boats, but all the more interesting for kayaks.) Tourism in the area is fairly understated: a few RV parks/campgrounds along the lone road that winds up the point, several surprisingly good restaurants, and La Bufadora, a tidal blowhole that sprays a geyser of seawater up into a Y-shaped cleft on the steep and rocky southern shore.

Most visitors are Mexicans, usually enjoying a weekend excursion to the blowhole. Most of the U.S. tourists who swarm south stop just short of Punta Banda, preferring instead the nightlife and local color of Ensenada. Those that do visit usually keep to the campgrounds at Punta Banda's base, leaving the long rocky arm and the distant islands peaceful and relatively undisturbed.

The wildlife has no doubt been affected by man's presence, but there is still much to see: from bright purple sea urchins on the ocean floor to gregarious sea lions basking on offshore rocks. Birds abound on the offshore islands. The water is chilly but snorkeling is good.

My favorite part, though, is the view. Less than an hour after launching at La Jolla, with the campgrounds and beaches and bustle of Ensenada left behind, one would hardly guess that the border is so near. The emerald-colored water undulates with gentle ocean swells rolling in from the northwest. The mist-enshrouded bluffs of Punta Banda tumble spectacularly into the bay. A fisherman, wearing only cut-off shorts, lowers himself by rope from a crumbly precipice to cast out a line from a remote and rocky beach below.

Starting Point: La Jolla

A large, private campground and RV park at La Jolla (also spelled La Joya) offers access to the wide, shallow-slope beach at the head of Bahía de Todos Santos. Just $7 per 2 persons entitles you to a basic campsite, toilets, and hot showers. A stony hill just past the tent sites drops down to the beach. A small grocery store and a mechanic are on the premises. Fellow campers, both Americans and Mexicans, can be very noisy: these are generally weekend partyers, not necessarily nature-lovers. Planning a trip for midweek would be smart. Management is friendly and probably amenable to your leaving your car parked here while you kayak the route. Camp Villarino, just down the road, has similar services and rates.

Long before there were campgrounds here, there was a shore whaling station, one of the few along the Baja coast. Shore whaling involved pursuing a whale from a boat launched from shore, usually no farther than 10 miles, and then towing the captured whale back to shore for processing. The station near La Jolla was in operation from 1868 to 1885, catching mostly gray and humpback whales.

Northern Shore of Punta Banda

As you proceed along the point, the coast quickly changes from low beachfront to rocky bluffs. Upon setting out one can immediately see El Rincón, meaning "corner," a square-shaped bluff. There are several very small potential landing sites before El Rincón, including a V-shaped pebble beach, accessible on land by a small dirt road, that might provide an alternative camping and launching site. El Rincón is reached just before mile 1.

Three humps in the distance form the next landmark, at mile 2. These rocks, just offshore, are the Tres Hermanas or "Three Sisters" (or three brothers, depending on whom you ask). On the way, some more hidden offshore rocks come into view; jagged, dark-colored and scored with crevices, these rocks make for good exploring. In calm seas, a kayak can navigate the passage between the rocks and the coast, and poke around some small sea caves just ahead.

Directly past Tres Hermanas is a large, stony beach, backed by bluffs. Above and ahead, sheer-faced reddish bluffs alternate with more gently sloping hills covered with green vegetation. The rocky spine of Punta Banda gains elevation as it climbs toward Pico Banda, at 1260 feet, its highest point. The spine, composed of metavolcanic rock, was pushed out into the Pacific by movement along the Agua Blanca Fault, a fault that is still active and was responsible for a small earthquake in 1991.

A Mexican couple may be sunning on the occasional near-shore boulder, their children visible as neon snorkels circumnavigating the rock in slow zigzags and the occasional splash of a rubber fin. One wonders, eyeing the steep bluffs of the coast's shore: How did they get there? Do they, like the fishermen, rappel by rope down to a favorite, hidden spot? Or are there, more likely, awkward paths winding past shrub and falling rock to the water's edge?

A small stone beach before the lighthouse, near mile 4.5, provides a place to stop and stretch at the end of Punta Banda, and perhaps clamber up a bluff to get an impressive view. Lush, fragrant plants, agaves and other succulents blanket the bluff tops, and a mysterious-looking cave invites exploration farther inland. From this stop one may survey the swells and fog and decide whether to cross to the Todos Santos islands, or shorten the trip by continuing around the point.

Dave Seymour, Glenn Pinson, Jan Richardson and John Reseck completed an expedition along the entire Pacific coast of Baja in the summer of 1992, the first time such a trip was done in double kayaks

Todos Santos Islands

Never a fan of long, open crossings, I was relieved on my first trip to Punta Banda to see how close the islands appeared. I was a bit confused, however, by how many islands there were; well over ten, it seemed, when I was certain that the Todos Santos Islands were only two. What I was seeing were the many islets and large offshore rocks that dot the end of Punta Banda. The blurry outline materializing from a distant veil of fog behind them was the true Todos Santos islands. Clear days are better for the crossing, obviously; but on both clear and overcast days take compass readings in case the fog thickens and obscures the islands entirely.

Those many islets I mistook for islands have another surprise of their own: sea lions. They're most abundant on the western side of the islet chain, and they may even follow you for a bit if they're feeling curious.

The crossing to the Todos Santos islands is just under 4 miles, taking on a calm day of slow but steady paddling a little less than 2 hours. Along this route I've spotted an enormous pod of common dolphins, their dark fins arcing through the swells as far as the horizon, as well as brown pelicans skimming the water's surface, and stray sea lions. Your paddle might also bump into an odd type of large, floating seaweed common here: bull kelp. It resembles a torpedo or an elongated buoy in shape, with one end rounded and fringed with leaves and the other trailing a thick, rubber-hose-like extension.

The Todos Santos islands are composed of the same rock as Punta Banda, and are similar in their rugged topography. Isla Sur, the southern island (also known as Isla Sureste) is the larger of the two, with flat-topped bluffs peaking at over 300 feet on the island's southern end. Isla

Norte (also known as Isla Noroeste) has lower bluffs, levelling out at about 50 feet.

Isla Sur is most kayakers' destination, not only because it is the larger and more interesting of the two islands, but also because, unlike landing on Isla Norte, landing on Isla Sur doesn't require a permit from the naval commander in Ensenada.

Approaching Isla Sur, one will see a white light tower perched on a hill to the left, and a larger, rounded hill to the right. Between these, a rocky, bird-limed landing area that supports several fish-camp shacks is reached at mile 9.

Along the southeastern side of the island are several small, rocky coves. Towering offshore rocks, many of them whitened with bird lime, begin about midway along the eastern side, creating a wide, beautiful channel navigable by kayak. Gulls, pelicans, cormorants and osprey dart overhead, or nest on the island's flat-topped bluffs; and the persistent call of the oystercatcher echoes from the shore.

At the northeastern side of the island are three large coves. The second of these is used by anchoring boaters. The third cove, with its wide, sheltered landing area, is frequented by kayakers and reached at mile 10. A climb from the pebble and cobble beach at the back of this cove leads up an easily scaled bluff to an area of low, even vegetation. This area is popular as a tent site; in fact, you may find someone here before you. Keep to the small area atop the bluff most commonly used for camping; don't tramp around farther inland or you may disturb the many birds that roost and nest on the islands. To prevent floataways, kayaks should be hoisted up to the blufftop during high tides, or tied securely to a rock.

From this campsite one has a magnificent view of the clear waters of the cove below, at the northeastern tip of the island, and the more turbulent surf crashing on the coast of the northern side of the island. Sea lions often swim around this point, popping their heads above water level to eye any activity on shore. The shallow ocean floor in this northeasternmost cove is brightly colored with red sea stars and purple sea urchins; kelp is thick in the passages between offshore rocks, and bright orange fish dart into sea caves near the entrance to the cove.

Kayakers should use caution circling the island from this point. The channel between Isla Sur and Isla Norte is very shallow and often turbulent. Refraction and confused waves abound all along the north and west sides of Isla Sur. Waves are biggest between November and February, and surfers have coined scary names like "Killer's," "Martillo" (The Hammer) or worse, "Thor's Hammer," for the breaks that occur when large, deep-water swells hit the northwest corners of both islands.

Finally, kayakers should be cautioned that there aren't as many good landing sites on these islands' western sides. Small coves, like the one at the very southwestern tip of Isla Sur, invite surge. In fact, my partner was carried the last few yards into this cove so quickly that he almost ran over a sea lion. The sea lion stuck around for a while, perhaps enjoying our frantic efforts to launch quickly and paddle our way back out.

Following seas are common on the return trip to Punta Banda, and swells passing between offshore rocks on the point's southern side create some quick currents. (Try zipping between the rocks off Cabo Banda for a simulation of whitewater kayaking.)

Just as one rounds the southern side of Punta Banda, at mile 16.5, there is a fine gravel beach with many small caves and holes punched into the rock along the shore.

The point north of Bahía Torrescano looks like a giant offshore rock joined by a spit of land. From Bahía Torrescano itself one can see a white structure at the top of a hill, as well as cars on the road that winds toward La Bufadora.

Bahía Papalote is easily identified by the many houses perched on its hills as soon as you enter the bay. La Bufadora is on the western side of the bay and is reached at mile 18.5. The blowhole becomes most forceful with an incoming tide, gushing a thundering billow of spray. Tourists watch from a guard rail on a bluff high above the geyser-producing sea cave. One may approach within several feet in a kayak, but be careful of the strong surge that comes before and after each blow. Good samaritans still glowing from a trip to the islands may want to pick up a few of the styrofoam cups that careless tourists drop from above.

Finish: La Bufadora

Take-out is easiest at a boat launch at the center of the Bahía Papalote, just next to a dive shop. A $5/day parking lot is above and to the left through a gate. A short walk from the point leads to the main road, Highway 23, which winds from La Bufadora back to La Jolla and out to a junction with Highway 1. Two restaurant-bars, including El Dorado (good seafood; a complete meal is about $8–10) mark this junction.

A blue van/bus can be waved down at this point to take you back down to the base of Punta Banda for $1. The bus comes irregularly throughout the day; you might ask at the restaurant when it is due next. Hitching is also quite easy here.

Other Options

The estuary on the northern shore of Punta Banda offers a good paddle for winter birdwatchers.

A 4-mile hiking trail winds around the Pico Banda; the trail starts just off Highway 23, 1.5 miles north of La Bufadora.

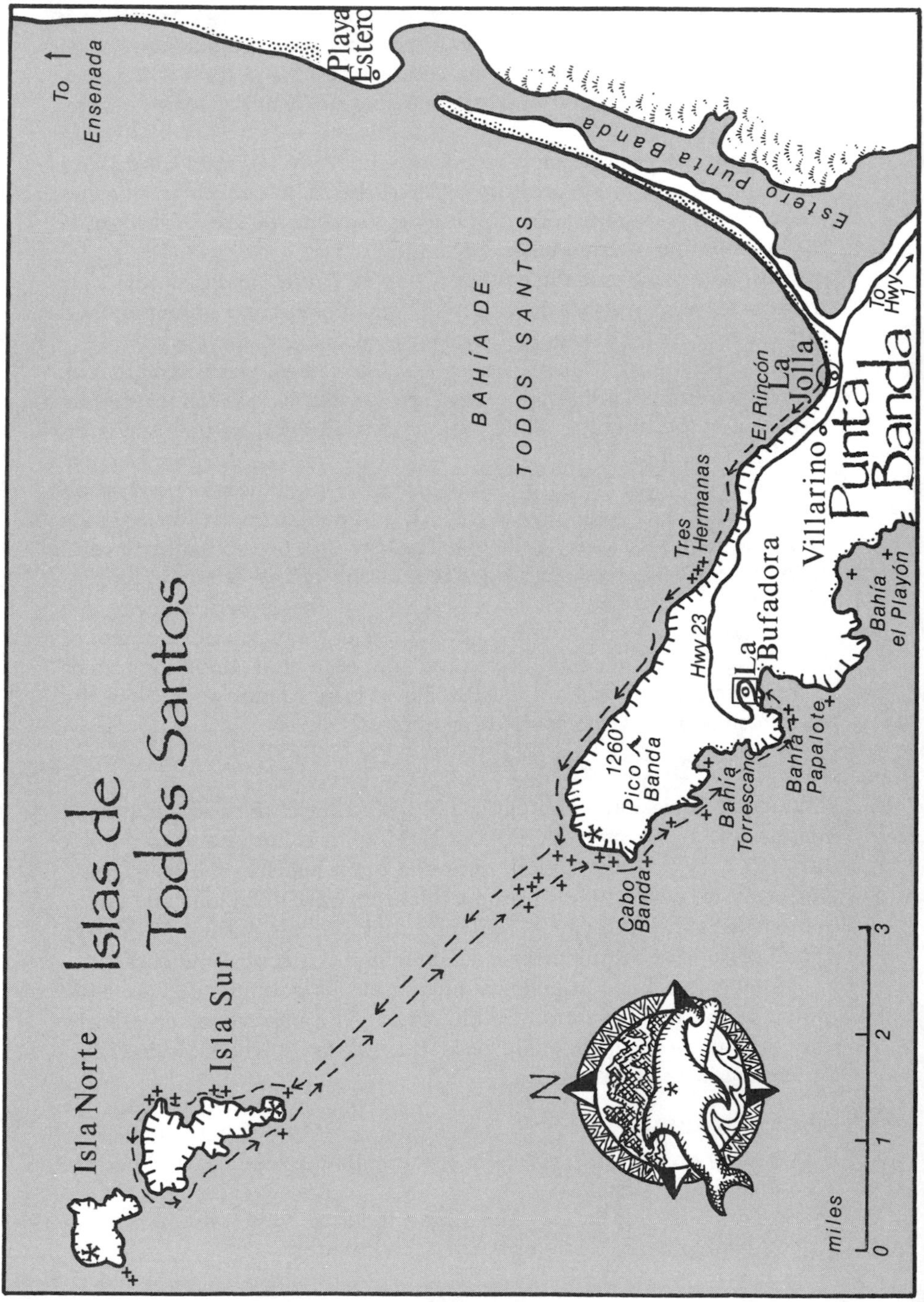

Islas de Todos Santos

Isla Norte

Isla Sur

To Ensenada

Playa Estero

Estero Punta Banda

BAHÍA DE TODOS SANTOS

El Rincón
La Jolla
Villarino
Punta Banda
To Hwy 1

Tres Hermanas

Hwy 23

1260 Pico Banda

La Bufadora

Bahía el Playón

Bahía Papalote

Bahía Torrescano

Cabo Banda

N

miles
0   1   2   3

ROUTE 2   San Quintín Bay: The Mudflat Nursery

Trip Summary: A 10-mile daytrip around a sheltered, shallow-water bay, renowned for the variety of its winter bird population and the gentle, understated beauty of its volcano-ringed western shore.

Trip Length: 1 day.

Charts: MEX Topo H11 B74 at 1:50,000

Getting There: San Quintín is 187 miles south of Tijuana, just off Highway 1; about a 5-hour drive from the border. To get to Bahía San Quintín, continue south on Highway 1 from the town of San Quintín for 4.7 miles, past the military camp and small town of Lázaro Cárdenas. At this point, Highway 1 will junction with several small dirt roads leading west to the Old Mill (Molino Viejo) and Old Pier (Muelle Viejo) motels (signs point the way). The bay itself is about 4 miles out along either of these roads.

Climate & Conditions: San Quintín has mild winters, with temperatures in the 50°s, and cool summers, with temperatures in the 70°s. Fog and overcast skies are common.

Water surface temperature ranges from 61° in winter to 66° in summer.

Wind is predominantly from the northwest at 5–6 knots, enough to make paddling into the wind sufficiently tiring: but, given the short fetch of the bay's interior, not effective in building up any large waves.

Like most of the Pacific, this route enjoys its most pleasant temperatures in the summer. However, for birdwatching, winter is clearly the optimal time.

"This is easy," my sister boasted as we set out on a 2-day tour of Bahía San Quintín, her first ever trip in a kayak. The wind was at our backs, the water calm. We barely had to paddle, concentrating instead on the scenery: old volcanic cones on the bay's west bank, protruding solemnly from a thin blanket of green scrub; old pier pilings and mill machinery, relics of the bay's wheat-farming days. At every point along the route we would be close to shore, paddling the sheltered waters of this nearly enclosed two-armed bay. No heavy swells, no difficult surf. A perfect trip, I reasoned, to introduce my sister to the sport.

We had a simple, pleasant paddle for most of the day, until we sought landfall. As soon as we'd set foot out of our kayaks, they would sink into deep, silty mud, the main component of Bahía San Quintín's shores. We would try another spot down the shore. And another. And another.

By dusk we were destitute. My sister's arms, unconditioned to the task, were aching. My ego, as a so-called experienced kayaker, wasn't in very good shape, either. Both of us were fed up with poling through the eel grass that choked the bay's shallows. The tide had receded, leaving

exposed sand bars that sabotaged our paddling, and an even longer zone
of wet muck between our boats and dry land. Our clothes were damp
and muddy, and we had both begun to shiver uncontrollably.

Resigned to setting up camp, we finally pulled up to a hopeful-look-
ing stretch of dark shore and stumbled wearily out of our kayaks.

We planted our feet upon the shore, witnessing with tired disap-
pointment the disappearance of our shoes into silty muck. We each lifted
one foot, smiling at each other nervously, and tried to high-step forward. This time, we both sank to our knees. A few panicky giggles broke
out as we struggled to free one leg, and then another, sinking further
with each step; finally, terrified screams erupting as our thighs sank
down into the ooze. We grappled for each other, wailing and flailing and
shaking, trapped in quick-mud, on the verge of hysteria, as the last reddish rays of sunlight silhouetted the volcanic peaks across the bay.

In the end, we escaped. By dropping to all fours, we were able to
spread out our weight on the quick-mud's surface, and crawl forward.
Unable to pull our boats up to dry land, we were nonetheless able to anchor them with weighted water bottles. A wet, muddy tent set up in a
scrub patch housed us until the next morning, when at high tide, we
were finally able to paddle away.

The moral of this story is simply a caution: beware Bahía San
Quintín's shallow mud flats. At low tide, they make coastal passage difficult, even for a boat as shallow-drafted as the kayak. For an ill-advised
camper, especially one racing against a setting sun, they can be rather
traumatic.

So why, given San Quintín's mucky, shallow nature, paddle there
at all? Because that same muck (and eel grass, as long as we're com-
plaining) attracts a bounty of wildlife. Fish, mollusks and crustaceans
thrive in it. Birds find it an attractive habitat, too. In fact, Bahía San
Quintín attracts more bird species than any other locale in Baja. Winter
is prime birdwatching time, attracting black brant, which feeds upon
the eel grass, as well as over 20 other species of ducks and geese. One
might also spot grebes, loons, egrets, herons, terns, owls, sandpipers,
plovers and others; a more specific, complete listing would tally over
100 species in all.

Outsmarting the mud flats is pretty simple, actually. Deeper waters run in a Y-shape extending into both arms of San Quintín Bay.
(The bay is actually divided into Bahía San Quintín, the east arm, and
Bahía Falsa, the west. The deeper parts of the channel join just south of
Volcán Ceniza where these two arms meet.) Keeping to this central part
of the bay means less scooting, poling and dragging. For exploration on
shore, wait for high tide, when the most daunting stretch of low-slope
mud flats will be underwater.

For camping, there are a few options. Scout a dry spot at high tide, avoiding the marshiest areas on the bay's east side. Similarly, land on Bahía Falsa's western shore (again, at high tide) and hike over to the Pacific side. Or finally, if you're an able enough kayaker to exit the bay, past the breakers that front the bay's southern entrance, you might scout for a good campsite just before the end of Punta Entrada. (At low tide sandbars in this area, as in much of the bay, are also exposed.)

These suggestions aside, the easiest and most enjoyable way to tour San Quintín Bay is to make a day trip of it. Take binoculars and identification books, leave the tent in the car, and be back before sunset to warm up or bed down at the Old Mill. In other words, leave the mud to the birds.

Starting Point: Old Mill Motel

In the late 1800s an English land company briefly settled the eastern shore of the Bahía San Quintín, establishing a grist mill, pier, customs house, cemetery and 19 miles of railway tracks. Their attempt to cultivate wheat was eventually foiled by drought, and the colony was abandoned. In his *Baja Boater's Guide*, Jack Williams mentions that the English land company once advertised the bay as capable of "holding all the fleets of Europe put together," an ambitious claim that you might find amusing as you paddle the small, shallow bay. Some of the mill machinery can still be viewed at the Old Mill Motel, as can pier pilings and remnants of the railroad causeway at the head of the bay.

Historical interest aside, the Old Mill Motel makes a good starting point because of its access to a small beach, boat launch and makeshift harbor area. Many American boaters frequent this launch, as well as the tastefully renovated and unusually well-stocked bar only a few meters away. (A rather pricey restaurant is also attached to the motel.) The parking lot behind the bar is quite convenient; you can probably arrange to leave your car here or at the Old Pier (Muelle Viejo) motel. Upon launching, you will notice an old structure on the west side of the bay; this is the old railroad causeway. In the distance are visible the six basalt craters that frame the bay, the nearest two being Cerro Kenton and Volcán Ceniza. A seventh crater in this grouping actually forms Isla San Martín, an island that lies outside the bay, in the open Pacific.

Proceeding for 1.5 miles, one comes to the camps of San Quintín, Mike María and Kin Mex. These are really no more than small clusters of ranch style homes, fronted by low (2–3 foot) bluffs and small patches of beach. Beyond lie low, scrub-covered hills.

You may cross strange white pipes and underwater grates as you paddle. These are utilized in the cultivation of oysters, an example of aquaculture being undertaken by a local cooperative.

To confine your paddle to a day trip, you will want to cross over to the eastern shore at about the 4-mile mark, when you are southeast of Volcán Ceniza. The eastern side of the shore is even shallower than the west, so tides will determine how closely you can hug it.

The old cemetery, part of the abandoned English settlement, lies here on the eastern shore at Mile 7. At Mile 9, one may easily paddle between the pilings of the Old Pier, which march by two's halfway across the bay. On shore the Old Pier Motel is visible; the Old Mill Motel lies 1 mile farther north.

Other Options

Advanced kayakers occasionally exit the bay, past the breakers that form at the bay's shallow entrance, and head northwest for nearly 10 miles to Isla San Martín.

Though not suitable for kayaking, the beach in front of the La Pinta Hotel (*outside* of Bahía San Quintín, further south along the coast) is popular. The beach here is windswept, the water cold and surfy; it's quite a different world from the inner shores of San Quintín, but better suited for camping. Think of stopping here before or after your kayak trip.

A view of a volcano behind the old mill machinery at Bahía San Quintín

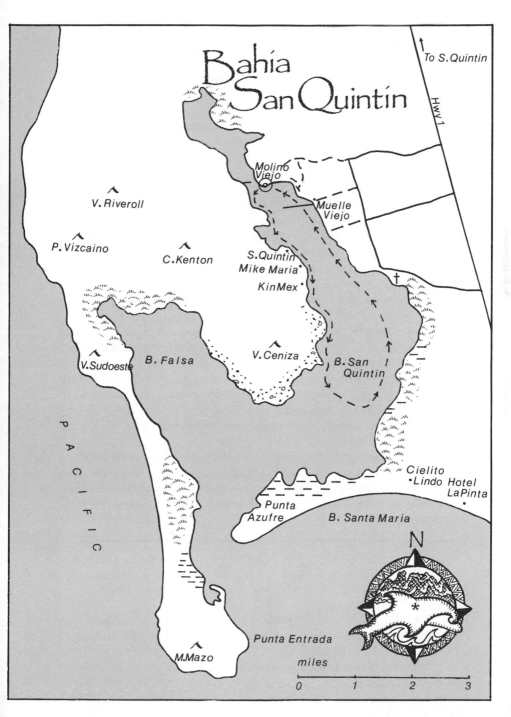

Bahía San Quintín

To S.Quintin

Hwy 1

Molino Viejo

V. Riveroll

Muelle Viejo

P. Vizcaino

C. Kenton

S.Quintin
Mike Maria
KinMex

V. Sudoeste

B. Falsa

V. Ceniza

B. San Quintin

PACIFIC

Cielito
Lindo Hotel
LaPinta

Punta
Azufre

B. Santa Maria

N

M.Mazo

Punta Entrada

miles

0   1   2   3

ROUTE 3   Magdalena Lagoons: The Inner Coast

Trip Summary: A 34 mile-trip through a long, narrow intracoastal waterway, between mangrove and sand dune shores; offering isolation, sheltered paddling, excellent birdwatching and frequent marine-mammal sighting.

Trip Length: 3–4 days.

Charts: MEX Topo G12 C46, G12 C56, & G12 C66 at 1:50,000

Getting There: Ciudad Insurgentes, a farming town of pop. 13,000, is 772 miles south of Tijuana via Highway 1. From here, a signed, paved road leads west 21.4 miles to the small port town of Puerto Adolfo López Mateos.

For a more scenic, adventurous drive, take the smooth dirt roads that lead west from Ciudad Constitución (16 miles south of Ciudad Insurgentes). Jackrabbits and quail abound on this route, which runs between irrigated fields alternating with stretches of picturesque desert. Ask for directions at the Conasupos (small, rural grocery stores) that spring up along the way.

When you see the water tower, you have arrived at Puerto López Mateos.

Climate & Conditions: The area is usually cool and overcast. Fog is common, usually dissipating by noon. Wind blows from the northwest, generally between 11 a.m. and 5 p.m., most persistently in spring. This wind can really whip up the dunes, blanketing every exposed surface with a layer of sand; expect to find sand in your pockets (and perhaps even your molars) for days after a trip.

Water surface temperatures range from 66° in winter to 75° in summer.

The short fetch in the lagoons prevents large waves from building up, but the wider part of Bahía Magdalena can create more challenging conditions, particularly in late afternoon. Use caution at Boca Soledad and Punta Entrada, both entry points to the open sea, where currents run swiftly.

My sleep was interrupted by an oddly urgent sound: a heaving sigh, a sonorous bellow from somewhere just beyond the tent's walls. It was not an alarm clock; not the whistleblow from the nearby López Mateos cannery.

I sat up, bleary-eyed. The sound repeated itself. And suddenly, I was out of the tent, running, pounding the shore of Isla Magdalena, trying to keep up with it.

The waters that wind through this narrow passage, this saltwater lagoon that separates the Isla Magdalena from the mainland, are green and murky. The sky is gray, woollen, occasionally whitened by fog. The

waterway is so narrow that it resembles a river more than an errant fin-
gerling of sea. The main shore is so near one can make out the cannery's
dock, the white-and-red striped lighthouse, the pangas resting on the op-
posite shore.

Just ten feet off of Isla Magdalena, where the sand sloped down
sharply into opaque water, the bluish-gray body of a dolphin surfaced. A
steamy bellow rose from its blowhole again, its back arched, its dorsal
fin cut through the water. It swam parallel to the shore at a pace just
faster than I could sprint on hard-packed sand. When I would hit a soft
patch I'd slow down, panting, but then the dolphin would surface just
ahead of me, and I'd struggle to keep up again. I made it no farther than
a quarter mile. It continued on, for some 30 miles perhaps, to the point
where the Isla Magdalena ends, where the lagoons widen out to Mag-
dalena Bay, where beyond Punta Entrada lies an exit to the open sea.

Later that morning we packed up camp and followed suit in our
kayaks, heading south along the "inner coast," a barrier island configu-
ration that makes for sheltered paddling and unique, up-close wildlife
viewing. We made three easy days of it, camping on Isla Magdalena's
windswept dunes, winding past pungently scented mangrove shores
thick with birds; joined many more times by dolphins who, always
faster than we, raced ahead through the lagoons.

The Whales of Magdalena Bay

We were delighted to share our trip with dolphins, but it is a different
marine mammal for which this area is famous: the California gray
whale. The gray whale begins its annual migration from the Bering Sea
in October, arriving in Baja to mate and calve between December and
March. Its stopping points include Guerrero Negro, Scammon's Lagoon, Laguna San Ignacio, and Bahía Magdalena, a few whales continuing all the way to the Sea of Cortés.

Of the lagoons and bays frequented on the Pacific side, Magdalena
Bay has been the longest to hold out on any restrictions against individual boaters and kayakers venturing into its waters during whale season.
For that reason, Magdalena Bay and its northern lagoons have been
popular kayaking areas, and many organized tours visit the area at season's peak.

Currently, local officials are beginning to enact some prohibitions,
however. The level to which these have been enacted, and more important, enforced, is not certain. The rationale for any prohibitions is quite
clear and understandable: it has been suggested that some whales may
be altering their migration and calving patterns as a result of the traffic
or crowding caused by whalewatchers' activities.

Many "paddling with whales" tours are still being offered, but some of these tours may be deceptive. They usually do offer paddling through the lagoons, but when it comes time to come face-to-face with the grays, whalewatchers are loaded into motorized pangas and whisked away to the prime spots within the bay. This is done for several reasons. First, the whales seem to recognize the sound of a motor and may even approach particular pangas based on recognition, thus ensuring more encounters. Second, the whales may breach or bump a boat, particularly one that is difficult to detect; thus, the motor helps warn the whales from getting *too* close.

To sum things up: you may wish to visit Bahía Magdalena during whale season, but don't be crushed if you're asked to keep your kayak on top of your car. (If you see other people paddling, they may be doing so under a commercial license.) Pangas can be legally rented to see the whales, or, better yet, campsites can be set up from which to observe with even less direct disruption.

Alternately, I'd recommend that kayakers not forget about visiting Bahía Magdalena at other times of year; there is still much to see, wildlife included, and few others with whom to share the lagoons and bay after the whales have headed back home.

Starting Point: Puerto López Mateos

López Mateos is a dusty cannery town, seldom visited by tourists, except in spring when whalewatchers convene to catch a glimpse of the California gray. (Puerto San Carlos is the more popular and accessible site for whalewatching.) It is a quiet, self-sufficient community, with over seven small grocery stores, beer concession, town square, and police station. There was only one restaurant as of this writing, the "Ballena Gris" (Gray Whale), which was closed but may open during future whale seasons.

Each morning, the mournful cannery whistle blows, and women workers in pale blue dress uniforms can be seen walking to work, where they will pack sardines and tuna. The cannery itself is a large building on the north side of town, with a pier and parking lot/small boat launch to one side. This is the best spot to launch, but the lot is probably not secure enough for leaving a car behind.

Parking, in general, is a bit tricky in López Mateos. I have left my car in the care of the local police station, just off the town square. There are few other "public" areas, and no hotels or campgrounds; therefore, a private arrangement must be made if you are to leave your car behind while you paddle.

The Isla Magdalena Shore

The northern part of Isla Magdalena, just across from the cannery launch, is composed of sand dunes, crisscrossed with vines and dotted with tufts of dune grass. Constantly reshaped by wind and shifting sand, they are largely unvisited and still pristine. The opposite mainland shore is covered by labyrinthine stands of mangrove and brush; uninhabited and inhospitable for most of the region south of López Mateos.

Occasionally, fishermen in pangas will pass in the channel. Amazingly, given the confines of the narrow passage, one may also see large, solitary ships, usually proceeding toward the cannery. But besides these few vessels, one doesn't see many other people, particularly on the windswept island itself. The official name for the waterway is particularly apt: Canal La Soledad, or "Solitude Channel."

Throughout this channel, small mangrove islets abound, most of them unmarked on any map. Storm, tides and other natural processes reshape the channel, so that one can never be sure whether a thick hedge of mangrove growth is another long, thin unmarked islet or the opposite bank. For these reasons, finding landmarks can be difficult. Precision navigation is not as terribly crucial here as it is elsewhere, though; one simply continues heading south. It really feels much more like a lazy river trip through the bayou than a Baja sea-kayaking tour.

Hiking on the island's dunes is tempting, since one can manageably cover the short distance over to the surf-battered Pacific side. Do remember that dunes are very vulnerable, however; don't pull out any vegetation or set a tent on top of the grass.

Beachcombing may turn up some interesting finds; debris from as far as Japan has been known to wash up on Baja's Pacific coast. Numerous ships have also met their end on these shores. According to Walt Peterson in his *Baja Adventure Book*, more wrecks have occurred off of Islas Magdalena and Santa Margarita than anywhere else on the peninsula, and his book is worth reading (or re-reading) for a history of some of the more notable disasters.

The sand dunes on the Isla Magdalena side peter out around the 9.5 mile mark, giving way to impenetrable thickets of mangrove for the next 2.5 miles. If you're looking for a place to camp, stop now or be ready to push on for another hour. At this point the channel also widens from its previous half mile or so width to a 2–3 mile width, in the middle of which sit the small, thickly vegetated isles of San Gil and Pauquino. Several types of clams blanket the tidal flats of these low isles; you might load up a bag and head farther south along the Magdalena shore for a suitable clambake/camping spot.

A windswept dune in the Magdalena lagoons

A low hill marks the shore near mile 12.5. Camping is possible at a few spots in this area.

The wider stretch of channel starts funneling down toward a narrow bend near mile 15. A band of sandy shore appears on the mainland side of the channel. On the island side, a small pocket in the mangrove-lined shore may be a little confusing. Keep your kayak heading south, or you may detour into this dead end pocket, thinking it's the "way out of the funnel." A rusty buoy marking the path of the narrowing channel may also help you find your way.

At mile 17, the narrowed channel swings due west. Maps refer to this bend as La Curva del Diablo (The Curve of the Devil), perhaps because of the devilish difficulty posed by navigating one's way to and around it. Once you've paddled around the curve and are proceeding west, you might have figured out another reason behind the well-deserved name: for the next 2.5 miles, you will more likely than not be paddling directly into the wind. Go ahead and curse; the channel straightens out again by mile 19.

Whereas the northern portion of Isla Magdalena was primarily dunes alternating with occasional stretches of mangrove, from here south the mangroves reign supreme. There are still small stretches of sand, easily spotted from a distance, but these are several miles apart. Though sand may be preferable to campers, the mangroves are actually an amazing part of this ecosystem. Specially adapted to draw nutrients from the saltwater, their roots in turn provide homes for crustaceans and mollusks. The mangrove stands are alive with birds: frigatebirds, herons, egrets, cormorants and oystercatchers all hover over or poke through the roots.

Camping is possible at a stretch of sand at mile 20.

Proceeding along the densely vegetated shore, one comes to a secondary channel leading west to the Estero el Garratazo, at mile 24.5. Larger waves can build up in this area, since the estuary runs parallel to normal wind direction. At sunset, the view from the junction of these channels is breathtaking. The sun's rays shimmer on the wind-roiled estuarial waters, and slightly farther down the primary channel an isolated mound of white sand dunes breaks up the otherwise jungle-green mangrove shore.

This stretch of sand, at mile 25, makes for excellent camping. The waters fronting it are quite shallow, which may necessitate some scooting and dragging at low tide; on the positive side, there is excellent clamming at low tide as well. There is also some "buried treasure" at this site. I should know; it was my partner who lost it! (If anyone finds a silver wedding ring in the sand, please send it to the publisher.)

From here the lagoons begin to widen out again, just before merging into the bay. Keeping to the mainland side of the shore, one begins to head southeast. One enters Bahía Magdalena proper at mile 30. The wide bay does experience larger waves than the lagoons. Given the predominantly northwest/west wind direction, you will probably have following seas. A globe-shaped water tower, a dock and two long, white buildings are easily sighted as you paddle the final 4 miles to the town of Puerto San Carlos.

Finish: Puerto San Carlos

A commercial L-shaped dock and warehouse extend from the developed area visible as you paddle into Puerto San Carlos. A decent, if slightly muddy, landing spot can be reached by rounding (or going under) the dock and paddling to the undeveloped shore just beyond it. Watch out if you try to land a little too far down, off the backyard of the local marine post; Spanish signs request that people not land. (I know this because I landed in order to read them. The Marines and their many dogs were all friendly, but I suppose one shouldn't push it.)

The town center is a short walk from the shore. Several restaurants, a PEMEX, grocery stores, motel, medical clinic and lively public square are in town.

An alternative landing site is at the Magdalena Fishing Village, a tourist complex southeast along the shore, just past San Carlos. The village is composed of a restaurant, some tourist cabins, and RV spots.

Puerto San Carlos is connected to the main highway by bus service. Hitchhiking is also very easy and common here; head toward Route 22, just northwest of the town center.

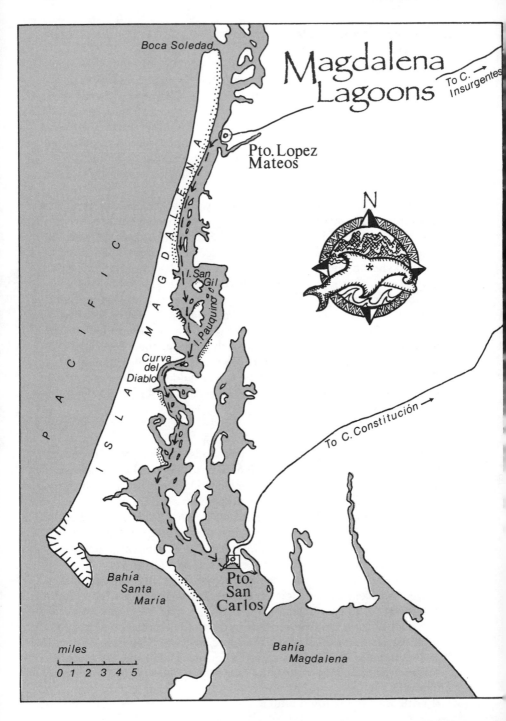

Chapter 5

The Northern Cortés

ROUTE 4   San Felipe to Puertecitos: From Taco Stands to Tidepools

Trip Summary: A 52.5-mile trip along the tide-scoured northern Cortés coast, a region of endless dunes, wide desert plains and a curious blend of cross-border cultures.

Trip Length: 4–6 days.

Charts: MEX Topo H11 B47, H11 B57, H11 B67, H11 B77 at 1:50,000

Getting There: San Felipe can be reached a number of ways from the border—by crossing over at Tijuana, Tecate, Mexicali or San Luís (south of Yuma, AZ). The most direct route is Mexicali to San Felipe via Highway 5, a trip of 123.6 miles. Highway 5 is well-paved and signed, similar in condition to Highway 1 but with significantly less traffic. San Felipe's main waterfront street is the Paseo de Cortés.

Bus service runs between San Felipe and both Mexicali and Ensenada but does not continue south to Puertecitos. The road from San Felipe to Puertecitos was once notoriously bad but now is paved and quite suitable for normal passenger cars. Dune buggies probably outnumber passenger cars from San Felipe south, and may be able to help out with short rides. Hitchhiking out of Puertecitos is possible but not common.

Note: Car storage is available at the Estrella del Mar storage facility, just behind the ABC bus station on Avenida Camino del Sur in San Felipe.

Climate & Conditions: The northern Cortés is a place of extremes. In the winter, daytime temperatures are in the 50–60°s, while summer temperatures can exceed 110°. In the wide, open spaces of the northern Cortés, shade is hard to find, and sunstroke and dehydration are serious summertime risks.

San Felipe receives less than 2 inches of rain per year. Sea surface temperatures range from 57° in January to 68° in July.

Winds are from the northwest from November to May, exceptionally strong spells of northerly winter winds requiring extra flexibility in trip planning. The rest of the year, winds are more gentle and variable; usually from the southeast, although stronger spells of wind can blow from the west or north. Generally, winds start picking up after 11:00 a.m. and blow until about 5:00 p.m., yielding to gentle breezes with the onset of evening.

The sea is a living, shifting, changing beast, and there is no place better to learn that fact than on the San Felipe–Puertecitos route. Twice a day this region experiences the second highest tides in the world, up to 22 feet, and any coastal observer witnesses first-hand that interplay of moon, gravity and racing water that hourly changes the landscape of the northern Cortés.

For almost any visiting boater other than a kayaker, this natural phenomenon would be a nightmare. But in the northern Cortés, the mobile kayaker has a crucial advantage. Unlike motorboats (or certainly, yachts!) the kayak can easily be hauled up to higher ground before a rising tide, or hauled down a beach and back into the sea when the tide has waned and left a long, dry expanse of sand. The kayaker is exempt from the serious problems of running aground, being landlocked, or needing to seek anchorage in a shifting sea. Of course, tidal calculations are still very important to prevent a campsite from being set up in advance of a tide or, more commonly, from necessitating a long (as much as ½ mile in some parts) and backbreaking kayak haul to the water in the morning.

With proper planning and accurate tide charts, however, the tides are a spectacular feature of touring in this region. Twice a day the tides creep up, chasing man and beast to higher ground, and then reverse and wane, leaving behind shallow pools of the sea's orphaned creatures: sea stars, crabs, clams, sand dollars and the occasional tiny octopus. The amateur naturalist or beachcomber is treated to a rare opportunity to study marine life just outside his or her tent. And, best of all, the kayaker truly learns what it means to live with the rhythms of the sea.

Starting Point: San Felipe

San Felipe, a town of about 11,000 residents, is a just-across-the-border tourist spot; and though it profits from the weekend parade of American partygoers, it also bears a sort of extended hangover from the pains of that trade. There are taco stands and 2-for-1 margarita deals, but there are also broken glass and dunebuggies zipping along the beach and fireworks whistling overhead just when you're trying to sleep.

Development has brought telephones and good roads, but also the need to be more careful not to leave gear unattended on the shore. Make no mistake, San Felipe is no Tijuana (or Los Angeles, for that matter). It is small, and it is still pretty safe and friendly and crime-free. But it is also not a hideaway or a remote tropical paradise; especially not during Spring Break, when student crowds swarm.

Hence, San Felipe is best used as a launching point. Make the most of its easy coastal access, enjoy its bright clam cocktail stands along the Paseo de Cortés, and then be off for less well-trod ground further south along the coast.

There are two options for launching. A level, sandy beach lies just across from the main boardwalk downtown, on the shore of the Bahía San Felipe. Parking spots are plentiful on the Paseo, just feet from the beach, making kayak unloading easy. The rocky headland of Punta El Machorro, visible north of the beach, provides some shelter within the bay.

For less commotion and a more remote launch, try one of the many beaches south of town just off the Avenida Camino del Sur, the main route hugging the coast. Beach access here is changing weekly because of the many hotels and condominiums sprouting up along the coast, but finding a paved road linking the Camino del Sur to the waterfront is not difficult.

Launching at the downtown beach, one paddles south through the hotel zone (beaches are technically public but dominated by a handful of resorts and RV parks overlooking the sea). Subdivisions are extending their concrete tentacles south. Be on the lookout for jet skis, swimmers and pangas.

A small breakwater-enclosed harbor is at mile 2.0. Take a detour inside to check out a small, battered fleet of shrimp trawlers. Fishing effort had been drastically cut back as of 1992, as a result of orders from the mainland, increasing tourism's importance as one of Baja's primary industries.

The coast from this point south is dominated by wide stretches of sandy shore, backed in parts by low bluffs. The Sierra San Felipe provides a stunning backdrop but is a good 10–20 miles inland; quite different from Baja Sur, where steep escarpments drop directly into the sea. The relatively flat, vast coastal morphology makes distances difficult to ascertain and low points difficult to distinguish from the cockpit of a kayak.

Miles 2–9 south of San Felipe are fairly developed and under construction. Between miles 9 and 10 the Hotel Fiesta and a terraced RV park are visible from sea.

At Punta Estrella, a low, marginal point at mile 10, the coastline turns south and most development peters out to intermittent American camps. About a mile inland, the Cerro Punta Estrella, a prominent ridge, extends for 4 miles south. The road heads inland as well, making access by car more difficult. Dunebuggies have their heyday here; tents and kayaks may be directly in the traffic path. This becomes less of a problem as one gets farther south.

A marvelous sight on the beaches south of Punta Estrella is the spawning of the grunion. This silvery, smeltlike fish comes ashore several evenings following the full moons of March, April, May and June. Just before dusk, during the high spring tide, the female grunion burrows into the sand and deposits her eggs. The male follows suit, fertilizing them as he wriggles into the sand. Chasing the grunion is a slippery, fun pastime and can yield a fried fish dinner.

When the tide recedes, a band of rocky shore is revealed, and brittle stars and other tidepool residents are plentiful. Fishing in this region yields corvinas and croakers, the latter living up to its name by making a distinct froglike noise when caught. The most common fish the non-fisherman will see is the mullet. Especially active just before dusk, the silvery fish leaps out of the water ahead of one's kayak, perhaps mistaking it for a predator.

A marginal point, Punta Diggs, is at mile 14.5 At mile 18, a camp lies at the entrance of a narrow tidal estuary, the Estero Pércebu. When the tide is out, the estuary is dry and difficult to distinguish. When flooded, a narrow finger of saltwater extends up to 2 miles south, hidden behind the dunes. Sand dollars abound here.

At mile 22.5, the Laguna Pércebu forms a small pocket in the shore. This entire area, between Estero and Laguna Pércebu, is one of periodic inundation. There is still sandy beachfront most of the way, but a short hike over the dunes reveals inlets of saltwater, small lagoons and generally briny, scrub-pocked muck. In at least one area, safely away from the beach, fist-sized holes appear in the prehistoric-looking muck, and at least a few of these holes harbor furry tarantulas. The area also looks to be appealing to snakes.

Bahía Santa María is a beautiful, shallow, crescent-shaped bay flanked by sandbars at mile 23.5. When the tide races out, most of the bay is dry, and the coastline appears straight. A camp is on the south side of the bay. My longest encounter with dolphins occurred here, at flood tide, as two bottlenoses chased small fish in and around the bay for over an hour.

From miles 24 to 36 is an almost continuous string of camps. Most of them are quite small, consisting of RVs or stone rotundas, and though numerous, are set back far enough to leave most of the shore clear and unfettered by anything but sand, dunes and gravel. If you establish yourself in what the camp considers its "territory," you may be asked to pay a small camping fee, though I've spent days on end camping in this area without seeing or being approached by anyone. The easiest way out of a conflict is to pay or move just a little farther south.

The camps are difficult to make out from sea, and only by going for a short hike inland can one usually tell them apart. Most of the residents of the camps are seasonal, and nearly all are Americans who rent their plots from local Mexican *ejidos*. Few of the camps have any facilities of interest to kayakers. Each camp is linked with the main road by sideroads of 0.5–1 mile, should you need to get back to a larger camp or a town for assistance. Only a few of them are named below.

Campo El Vergel is a sizeable camp at mile 27. A white light tower poised atop low bluffs is a dependable landmark. Inland from the camp, just south of where it links up with the main road, are a store and a medical clinic; a good mid-route stop for restocking supplies. Canned goods, bread, staples and snacks are sold, as well as water and propane.

Playa Campo Cadena is at mile 31. Campo Mar y Sol is at mile 33. El Coloradito is at mile 35.5.

From this point south, the beach becomes rockier, and the transition from sand to gravel, pebbles and cobbles translates to fewer beach camps and a wilder, less-often-visited stretch of terrain. A few camps still exist, but they are fewer, smaller and farther spaced than those above. Small Mexican fish camps become more common as one proceeds south. The main road swings farther inland at this point, rejoining the coast just north of Puertecitos.

At mile 47, just past a marginal point called Punta San Fermin, is a dark light tower. A small Mexican fish camp is set back from the shore. Just inland are the *campos* El Zimarrón and La Violeta.

There are two ways to land at Puertecitos. The first of these is North Beach, a gravelly, shallow cove on the north side of the rocky Puertecitos peninsula at mile 50.5. Pangas line the west side of the cove, and an odd, pyramid-shaped house was recently under construction atop a sandy bluff on the east shore of the cove. The beach is a bit fishy and swarming with gulls, but camping is possible. From this point, a dirt road leads 1 mile south past a dusty airstrip and into the center of town.

The second and better way to land at Puertecitos is to paddle 2 more miles around to the southern cove. En route one sees American houses perched on rocky bluffs. A hotspring is located near the end of the rocky point forming the cove's eastern boundary; the temperatures of the small pools vary with the incoming tides. A launch ramp and breakwater are just inside the point. The cove itself is mostly shoals, and dries at low tide. The head of the cove has a sand beach, and landing here deposits you, at mile 52.5, in front of the few buildings which constitute "downtown" Puertecitos.

Finish: Puertecitos

The beauty of Puertecitos lies in the eye of the beholder, though one's mode of transport plays a large role as well. If you arrive by car or plane, the town looks dirty and forlorn; a graveyard of rusted-out car bodies, stolen street signs and old tires. If you arrive by kayak, however, after nearly a week of paddling, Puertecitos has a gritty, rustic appeal. On my first trip to Baja, I found it to be a bizarre and charming place, full of interesting characters—both Mexican and American—friendly albeit mangy camp dogs, and a welcome supply of tacos, cold drinks and camaraderie.

Americans and Mexicans co-exist in Puertecitos. The Americans stick to the bluffs running along both sides of town; the Mexicans live mainly in shacks and converted trailer and bus homes along the town's flat, central strip. The Palapa, a rotunda-shaped bar on the south beach, serves a limited stock of drinks (Coke and beer, usually) to both groups and comes to life with heated games of pool (on a sloping table) or the occasional cantina-style scrap. A small motel with surprisingly pretty rooms, a gift shop and a minimal-menu restaurant (with sporadic hours and no beverages—bring your own from the bar) are next door. A PE-MEX is just behind this complex; its supply of fuel is unreliable.

Further north of this "Zona Turística," along a handful of dusty roads, is the Alfabeta a grocery store, stocked with canned goods, staples, fruits, vegetables and snack foods. Letters can be left in a phone-booth-turned-post office behind the Palapa; local residents transport them to the border for mailing. Water and tortillas are sold from houses or trailers in town; ask at the grocery store for directions. The town darkens quite suddenly at 10 p.m. When the generator gets cut; be prepared with a flashlight if you're not safely tucked away in your tent.

Other Options

A shorter trip could easily be planned by launching at Punta Estrella and arranging for pick-up or shuttle at one of the camps farther south, though be sure to choose a camp with reliable landmarks. From Punta Estrella to Campo El Vergel (site of a lighthouse), for instance, is 17 miles.

The brown pelican was nearly wiped out by DDT, but now it thrives along the Baja coast

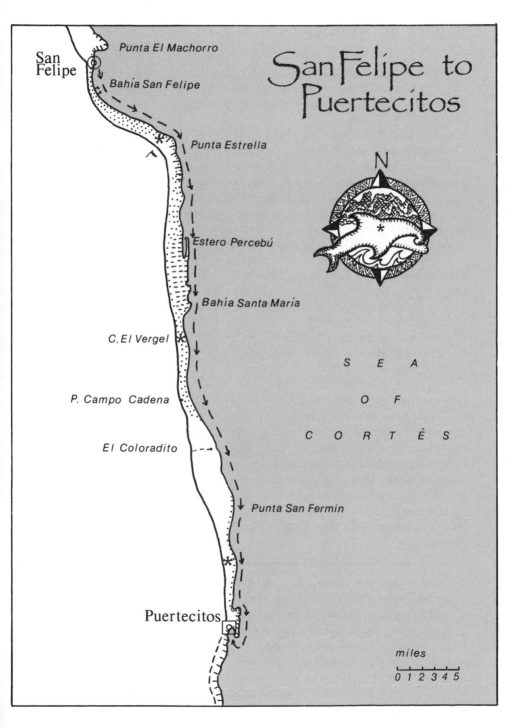

San Felipe

Punta El Machorro

Bahía San Felipe

Punta Estrella

Estero Percebú

Bahía Santa María

C. El Vergel

P. Campo Cadena

El Coloradito

Punta San Fermin

Puertecitos

San Felipe to Puertecitos

N

SEA

OF

CORTÉS

miles
0 1 2 3 4 5

ROUTE 5 Puertecitos to Huérfanito: A Glimpse of the Rugged North

Trip Summary: A 17-mile trip along a rocky, stark and less-visited part of the northern Cortés coast, offering isolation, opportunities for fishing and fossil-hunting, and views of an extinct volcano.

Trip Length: 2–3 days

Charts: MEX TOPO H11 B77, H11 B88 at 1:50,000

Getting There: San Felipe is 123.6 miles south of Mexicali via Highway 5, a well-paved and well-signed highway. The road from San Felipe to Puerticitos was once notoriously bad, but now the 52-mile trip is suitable for normal passenger cars. From Puertecitos south to Huérfanito, the road abruptly deteriorates and is suitable only for 4-wheel-drive vehicles. I know people who have made it in small, low-clearance cars but mine couldn't make it, especially with kayak gear loading it down.

There are no buses or public transport south of San Felipe, and even regular car traffic slows to a trickle south of Puertecitos. Hitchhiking may be possible, but not common. Unless you have a vehicle waiting to shuttle you out, or plan to continue south, you'll probably have to do a round-trip back to Puertecitos.

Climate & Conditions: The northern Cortés is a place of extremes. In the winter, daytime temperatures are in the 50–60°s, while summer temperatures can exceed 110°.

The area receives less than 2 inches of rain per year. Sea surface temperatures range from 57° in January to 68° in July.

Winds are from the northwest from November to May, exceptionally strong spells of northerly winter winds requiring extra flexibility in trip planning. The rest of the year, winds are more variable, usually from the southeast, although stronger spells of wind can blow from the west or north. Westerly gusts are especially prevalent in the Volcán Prieto area, often continuing through the night.

Generally, however, winds start picking up after 11:00 a.m. and blow until about 5:00 p.m., yielding to gentle breezes with the onset of evening.

The coast south of Puertecitos is stark, steep and rocky. The flat vistas, the endless sandy stretches that predominated from San Felipe south are now abruptly obliterated by the encroachment of a mountain range, the Sierra Santa Isabel. As soon as one has left the shelter of Puertecitos's diminutive southern cove, towering bluffs rise up to flank the shore. Here, for the first time along the northern Cortés coast, shadows are cast upon the water.

This change is not only scenic. Population and development are much less in this area: building and living here are more difficult than in the dune camps of the level north. The road that parallels the coast was once Baja's worst; now, even in its improved condition, it's not much more than a tortuous, rubble-strewn scar. In places it swings inland abruptly, leaving miles of rocky coast inaccessible except by boat. Not many sailboats come this far north, and only a handful of motorboats consider it worth the gas money to fish in these parts. This area is not the most remote in Baja, but considering its proximity to the border and the tourist center of San Felipe, its degree of isolation is remarkable. Between Puertecitos and Huérfanito, one will probably see more pelicans than tourists, more dolphins than fishermen, more rock-roaches than human residents.

Rock-roaches? Well, perhaps I should explain that last part. A rock-roach is more properly known as a rock louse, or Ligia occidentalis. *It is a harmless little scavenger of algae that lives in the littoral zone and spends its days harmlessly gnawing away and waving its antennae, always just inches ahead of an incoming tide or inches behind a receding one. It doesn't seem to bite, sting, go after humans or do anything but scamper over the rocks.*

Kayakers will encounter members of the Ligia occidentalis *species along much of Baja, but its sudden appearance and abundance here say much about the shoreline of this area. The impressive tides of the northern Cortés are still critical here, giving the* Ligia *a lot of littoral to explore. But rather than wide, sandy beaches, the receding tides now bare great rocky or boulderous bands of shore, great for scavenging and scampering, but not so great for landing, launching or portaging a kayak.*

This problem zone is especially noticeable in the area surrounding Volcán Prieto, the dark, looming, extinct volcano that is one of the highlights of this route. If one lands and launches at high tide, one can pull directly up to a pebble-and-sand beach suitable for camping just next to the volcano. If one tries to land or launch at low tide, one faces a hike along slippery, volcanic sharp-edged, barnacle-encrusted boulders that may extend the length of a football field. Timing is critical. One may choose not to land here but the same problem exists, to a lesser degree, in much of the northern Cortés.

The tides, the rocks, the mountains, the remoteness all contribute to an ambience that is raw and rugged but also invigorating. Along this coast, one is reminded of the true nature of Baja: a peninsula violently born of shifting plates, straining faults, and spewing volcanos. A coyote howls, a canyon echoes, a fossil is found imprinted in stone, and one feels all the more alone in this place.

Starting Point: Puertecitos

Puertecitos is a small, rustic town inhabited by both Mexicans and Americans, visited occasionally by fishermen, pilots, and hardy drivers heading farther south to the Islas Encantadas or Gonzaga Bay. Services are minimal, including a bar called The Palapa, a small restaurant, a grocery store, unreliable PEMEX, a motel and an airstrip. Water and tortillas can be purchased at two people's homes; inquire in town. For a more complete description, see the San Felipe–Puertecitos route above.

There aren't any established public places safe for leaving a car. You might try making arrangements with a resident in town or at a camp or RV park just north of town to leave your car in a private, watched spot.

Launching points include the North Beach, north of town, and the beach directly behind The Palapa on the town's southern cove. The southern cove dries partially at low tide.

From Puertecitos, one can make out the first few islands of the Encantada chain nearly 20 miles south; Huérfanito, the small light islet; Muerto, the darker, large island; and Lobos, a white island that catches the light and is visible from quite a distance.

Launching from the southern cove, one paddles past the first dark, cliffy point at mile 0.75, with rocky bluffs continuing south. There aren't many good landing or camping spots, although one fairly deep niche just past mile 2 has an adequate pebble-cobble beach. Good tidepools are the best reason for stopping at this secluded, rocky spot.

Fishing for corvina, bass and grouper is good in this area. A frequent sight on shore are the remains of triggerfish, a good eating fish with horselike teeth and an amazingly tough, leathery skin.

A stretch of sand-and-gravel beach is at mile 3. A better one is at the back of a pretty cove at mile 5, the site of a small camp, Playa La Costilla. Past Playa La Costilla is a low point with a broad, sandy shore. A line of surf breaks off this point.

The Volcán Prieto provides an unmistakable landmark from mile 9–10. The "Dark Volcano," no longer active, has a sheer eastern face that drops directly into the sea. Dolphins are frequently sighted here. A nearby resident reportedly found a well-preserved ammonite fossil near the volcano and sold it to Johnny Carson for a tidy sum. The volcano is flanked by picturesque scrub desert and would make for an interesting hike, but watch out for the sharp volcanic boulders that expose at low tide; they're not very kind to the bottom of a kayak.

The last 6 miles of this route are the most stunning. The coast dips southwest near mile 10 and returns southeast at mile 12; between these points one feels encircled by the steep, multi-hued cliffs set flush against the shore.

Several small pebble beaches are formed at the bases of arroyos in this area; one of these is at mile 12.5. A small pebble beach is visible just before Punta Santa Isabel, a prominent point at mile 15.5.

The Isla Huérfanito, or "Orphan Island," is ½ mile offshore at mile 17. The rocky, bird-limed island is so named because it is cut off from the other Encantada Islands farther south. Very strong currents race between the island and the shore, with some turbulence and confused waves as the tides force their way through such a small space; use caution.

Finish: Huérfanito

The camp of Huérfanito is just across from the island. A small collection of houses, an airstrip and a few shade trees are visible from sea. Most of the residents are American, and several are retired military personnel who fly as if still in battle, buzzing the camp and its few crooked weathervanes.

A broad stretch of sand beach good for camping extends past the camp.

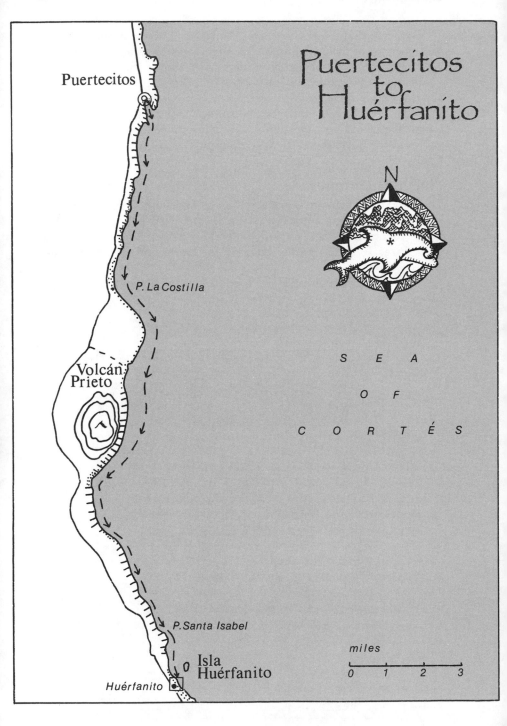

Puertecitos

Puertecitos
to
Huérfanito

N

P. La Costilla

Volcán
Prieto

S   E   A

O   F

C   O   R   T   É   S

P. Santa Isabel

Isla
Huérfanito

Huérfanito

miles

0   1   2   3

ROUTE 6   The Enchanted Isles

Trip Summary: An approximately 21-mile trip along the remote islet chain "Las Encantadas," following either of two possible routes: coastal paddling or island-hopping. From afar, the chain provides a picturesque and mysterious backdrop. Up close, seabirds, sea lions, and interesting geological origins characterize the isles.

Trip Length: 2–3 days

Charts: MEX Topo H11 B88, H11 D18 at 1:50,000

Getting There: Although the road from San Felipe to Puertecitos is suitable for normal passenger cars, it abruptly deteriorates from that point south. Continuing 17 miles south to Huérfanito is a task best undertaken with a 4-wheel-drive vehicle.

There are no buses or public transport in this area. Hitchhiking is difficult and not recommended. The handful of part-time residents and vacationers who visit the small camps from Huérfanito south often arrive by private plane.

Climate & Conditions: The northern Cortés is a place of extremes. Winter temperatures are in the 50°s, dipping down to the 40°s at night, while 100°+ days are the norm at summer's peak. The area receives less than 2 inches of rain per year. Sea surface temperatures range from 57° in January to 68° in July.

Winds are from the northwest from November to May, exceptionally strong spells of northerly winter winds requiring extra flexibility in trip planning. The rest of the year, winds are more variable, usually from the southeast, although stronger spells of wind can blow from the west or east.

"Islands too far off, according to the map, are visible; while others which should be nearby cannot be seen at all until they suddenly come bursting out of the mirage. The whole surrounding land is unsubstantial and changing."
                                                      — *John Steinbeck and Ed Ricketts*
                                                      The Log from the Sea of Cortez

   Steinbeck and Ricketts never made it as far north as the Encantadas, but this small chain of five islands in the northern gulf would have only confirmed their suspicions about the Cortés. Here, in the Encantadas, mirages are common. Landmarks shift and shimmer. The smallest of the isles occasionally rise up and levitate above the water's surface, a fine blue line of waves rolling underneath.
   In addition to these visual trickeries typical of many Cortés islands, the Encantadas have a few mysteries of their own: currents on their eastern and western sides run in opposite directions, rocks washed from their shores float. Navigation in the region is confounded by the fact

that no one is sure of the precise positions of each barren, sun-scorched isle. Official charts note their locations as "approximate" only.

The second island, Isla Muerto, is the most eery and compelling of the chain. It isn't just its name, "The Dead One," or its color, a brownish ochre that glows crimson in the rays of the setting sun. It's the way it follows you as you paddle, appearing forever due east even when the compass points north, as if no matter how hard you paddle it refuses to be dispatched. And it's the way it seems to get longer and longer, stretching both farther ahead and farther behind, until its parabolic silhouette seems to surround your craft.

At least, that's how Muerto appears from the coast. Nearer, perhaps, it may not seem so eery or mysterious. Nearer, perhaps, it is exposed as nothing more than a craggy, reddish rock dusted with bird lime.

In truth, I've never camped on the islands themselves, choosing to enjoy them from a distance. On my first visit, I was dissuaded from island-hopping by a spell of strong winds. Later, when I wanted to retrace the route, I asked a seabird expert about the nesting sites on the isles. He reported that they were in fact extremely sensitive to disruption, particularly on Isla San Luís, the island that is, unfortunately, the most suited to camping. Guidebooks mention that San Luís stinks and swarms with flies; well, no wonder, it's covered with guano!

In summary, then, there are two ways to paddle the Encantadas. Particularly in spring, when bird (and sea lion) populations are at their most sensitive, you can follow the coast, enjoying the spectacular views offered by the distant isles. Alternatively, the rest of the year, you can island-hop, planning your mileage so that you pass by but do not camp on Isla San Luís.

Starting Point: Huérfanito

The camp of El Huérfanito is just across from the island of that name. A small collection of houses, an airstrip and a few shade trees are visible from sea. Most of the residents are American.

The Isla Huérfanito, or "Orphan Island," is 0.5 mile offshore. The rocky, bird-limed islet is so named because it is cut off from the other Encantada Islands farther south. Very strong currents race between the island and the shore, with some turbulence and confused waves as the tides force their way through such a small space; use caution.

Route A: Coastal Paddling

Most of the coast is characterized by rock-and-cobble beaches backed by low, sandy bluffs. In a few locations the coast levels out slightly, bluffs moving far enough back to make room for broader beaches and more gently sloping camping sites. The foreshore in most places is com-

posed of cobbles and boulders, making for a potentially wearing portage and launch at extreme low tide; plan accordingly.

A broad sand beach extends south of the camp of Huérfanito,
quickly climbing to form low sandy bluffs, forcing the road inland. The
northern tip of Isla Muerto, stained powdery white, is due east of the
coast just past mile 3. Isla Lobos, a brilliantly white-stained islet visible
for many miles, is due east just before mile 6. The coast levels out again
after mile 6, broad pebble beaches providing good camping sites
backed by crumbly bluffs.

The stone foundation of a small hut, possibly left by a road-build-
ing brigade, can be found atop low bluffs near mile 6.5. Reportedly,
wherever the road builders stopped for any period of time, they deci-
mated the local oyster population. To find oysters on this route, then,
look for the steepest areas of shore, where the road swings inland and
the road crew had to satisfy themselves with bean and tortilla dinners.

Isla Encantada is due east at mile 9. Higher bluffs hug the shore
from mile 10 to 15. Landing is possible, but the boulder-and-porous-
cobble beaches are unsuited for camping. The northern tip of Isla San
Luís is due east at mile 11.5.

Thriving oyster beds can still be found between mile 15 and 16. On
our last trip, my partner and I headed to the water's edge with a bottle
of tabasco and a shucker, eating the rock oysters right on the spot. We
took the feast at least 10–20 oysters too far, and paid for it that night. We
tossed and groaned in sync as strange oyster nightmares troubled our
sleep.

A broad sand beach backed by sand bluffs extends between mile 16
and 17.5. A handful of houses stand behind the bluffs. The coast swings
east at mile 19. The beautiful fine-sand beach of Playa Bufeo extends
between miles 19 and 21, with an excellent view of the southern, striated face of Isla San Luís.

Route B: Island-hopping

The island crossings range from 2.5 to 3.5 miles, with minimal camping
sites on Isla Muerto. Landing is possible on Isla Encantada and the Islote Pomo just east of Isla San Luís; landing is possible, but discouraged,
on Isla San Luís. No landing is possible on Isla Lobos.

A broad sand beach extends south of the camp of Huérfanito,
quickly climbing to form low sandy bluffs, forcing the road inland. The
northern tip of Isla El Muerto, stained powdery white, is due east of the
coast just past mile 3. The crossing is just under 3 miles, and several
cobble-backed coves on the island's southwestern side provide possible
landing or camping spots.

The crossing from the tip of Muerto to Isla Lobos is 3 miles. "Lobos"
is the Spanish word for sea lion, the primary inhabitant of this small,

steep isle. From May to August, the male sea lions can be particularly territorial. Kayakers should give Isla Lobos a sufficient berth.

The crossing to Isla Encantada is 2.5 miles. A small, rocky beach permits landing at the islet's southwestern end. From the southern tip of Encantada to the Isla San Luís is a crossing of 2.5 miles. Several cobble-and-pumice beaches are on the island's east side. Walt Peterson, author of *The Baja Adventure Book*, explains that the semicircular bluff forming the island's eastern side was the inside curve of a volcano, and that the cone of dark lava in the center was the vent plug. Several of the islands in the Encantada chain are volcanic in origin, but at San Luís, those origins are most visible.

On the southwestern side of San Luís, a sandspit extends from the island, providing a nesting area for over 12,000 pelicans each year. This potential landing area, though convenient, could be very disruptive to the hordes of pelicans. Particularly from March to June, give this area a wide berth.

The final crossing, to Punta Bufeo directly south of Isla San Luís, is a paddle of 3.5 miles.

Finish: Punta Bufeo

A string of stone houses lines the beach at the American camp of Punta Bufeo, terminating at a dark, rocky point. Behind the houses are an airstrip and a small restaurant. Rental cabins may also be available.

Brian releases a porcupine fish from his trolling line

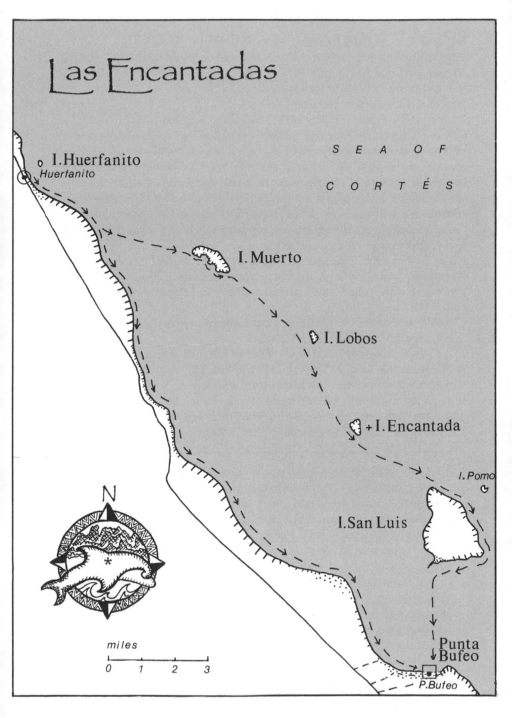

Las Encantadas

o I.Huerfanito
Huerfanito

S E A   O F

C O R T É S

I.Muerto

$) I. Lobos

$) +I.Encantada

I.Pomo
७

N

I.San Luis

Punta
Bufeo
P.Bufeo

miles

0   1   2   3

ROUTE 7   Gonzaga Bay: Remote Retreat

Trip Summary: A selection of 1- or 2-day trips, ranging from 6 miles to 30 miles, from a base camp in Gonzaga Bay, offers sheltered paddling and resort amenities in a remote setting.

Trip Length: 1–2 days per trip.

Charts: MEX Topo H11 D18, H11 D28, H11 D29 at 1:50,000

Getting There: Gonzaga Bay can be reached via a "4-wheel drive only" unpaved road from the north or the west. (Actually, many normal passenger cars make the trip; but at the very least, make sure your vehicle has high clearance.) Coming from the north, the camp of Alfonsina's, on the shore of Gonzaga Bay, is 46 miles from Puertecitos. From the west, Alfonsina's is 35 miles from the Highway 1 turnoff for Calamujué.

Hitchhiking is difficult and probably not recommended. Many visitors to the area arrive by private plane.

Note: In the past, Alfonsina's has hosted an annual Memorial Day weekend party that has drawn impressive crowds. If you're hoping for peace and quiet, plan your visit around any of the remaining 51 weekends of the year.

Climate & Conditions: Winter temperatures are in the 50–60°s. Summer temperatures are in the 90–100°s.

The area receives less than 2 inches of rain per year. Sea surface temperatures range from 57° in January to 68° in July.

Winds are from the northwest from November to May, with exceptionally strong spells of northerly winds in winter months. Gusting westerlies are also common. The rest of the year, winds are more variable, usually from the southwest to southeast.

It's hard to get to Gonzaga Bay. If you don't have the right kind of vehicle and nerves of steel, it's nearly impossible. And once you get there, there isn't much to do. There are no phones, mail, stores or tourist facilities other than the bare-bones establishments at Alfonsina's and Papa Fernandez's; just several miles of fine-sand beach, a barren island, a pristine, turquoise bay; and rocky headlands to the north and east. In other words, not a bad place to paddle, poke around and generally hide away for a few days.

Alfonsina's has been a noted refuge for a while now. The small resort celebrated its 25th anniversary with a bicultural bash in 1991, attracting celebrants from all corners of the world. ("Whoops, still on Moscow time," a pilot at the next table was overheard saying on our last visit.)

Even when there isn't a major fiesta in the works, distant visitors often arrive by private plane, touching down on the dusty airstrip that runs just behind the camp. Rusty plane parts and a dead body in the mountains behind the camp suggest that landing facilities here aren't the latest or the safest. The airstrip at Gonzaga Bay may in fact be the only airstrip you'll ever paddle, if you have that urge: at high tide, the strip has a tendency to flood.

If you're heading to a southern route, Gonzaga Bay makes a worthy detour. You can take a weekend and hone your skills by paddling the sheltered waters at the heart of the bay. If you're stringing together the northern Cortés routes, from San Felipe south, Gonzaga Bay makes an unbeatable final destination. You can relax and debrief before returning to the outside world.

Starting Point: Alfonsina's

The camp is composed of a small restaurant-motel and a string of American-owned residences running parallel to the airstrip, along a sandspit attached at low tide to the island of San Luís Gonzaga.

The restaurant dishes up surprisingly good food, particularly their fish and shrimp dinners. The motel rooms are cheap and basic: plywood walls and no private bathrooms. Water and staples can usually be bought at the resort, in limited quantities.

Good camping sites are available on the fine-sand beaches in front of the resort and all along the bay's shore.

Trip 1: Isla San Luís Gonzaga: 6 Miles Round-trip

A circumnavigation of the rocky island of San Luís Gonzaga (not to be confused with Isla San Luís of the Encantada chain) would make a good half-day paddle of 6 miles.

At low tide, the southwest corner of the island is connected to the camp of Alfonsina's by a sandbar (easily portaged). Across from the northwest corner of the island, on the main shore, is another small resort community named after its patriarch, Papa Fernandez. The bay fronting the resort, sheltered by the western half of Isla San Luís Gonzaga, is the Bahía Willard. The bay and the flooded area behind the Alfonsina's sandspit are good places to go clamming at the end of your trip.

Trip 2: Alfonsina's to Punta Bufeo: 9 Miles One-way

Launching at Alfonsina's, one paddles the western shore of Isla San Luís Gonzaga, taking a shortcut through Bahía Willard. Punta Willard, the bay's northern headland, is at mile 2.5. Beyond the rocky point, there is a fine stretch of fine-sand beach at mile 3. From this point, the coast begins to climb to rocky bluffs alternating with a few sandy landing areas. A light tower is at mile 4.

Sheer bluffs extend for most of the remaining shore all the way to the rugged promontory of Punta Bufeo, at mile 8.5. The emerald-colored water around the point is beautiful and clear, and snorkeling is excellent.

Several cobble niches in the bluffs permit landing and secluded camping, as well as bone-collecting; we found a nearly complete skeleton of what appeared to be a bobcat or related animal.

Rounding the point, the small camp of Punta Bufeo is visible at mile 9. Miles of fine-sand beaches with a view of the Islas Encantadas extend beyond the camp. A restaurant and an airstrip lie behind the row of American-owned stone houses; rental cabins may also be available.

Trip 3: Alfonsina's to Punta Final: 30 Miles Round-trip

The first mile of shore south of Alfonsina's is vacation-home territory. A string of approximately 60 residences, most of them American-owned, line the shore. A stretch of dunes extends from miles 2 to 5. The mountains are back from the shore in this area, fronted by a flattened plain.

At mile 5, a marginal point divides Bahía Gonzaga from Bahía San Francisquito to the east. Flat, sandy shore continues to mile 8, where the small American community of Punta Final is located. The village is smaller than Alfonsina's, with an airstrip and approximately 30 residences. Just past the village of Punta Final is a small islet connected to the land by a sandbar, which local residents call Snoopy. Many boaters, both American and Mexican, use this sandbar to launch and to land at low tide. You might be able to buy some fresh fish here if you time your visit right.

A double-headed cove east of the village, at mile 10.5, provides the best snorkeling and secluded landing spots in the area. Small beaches lie at the back of either side of the split cove.

The cliffy promontory of Punta Final is actually composed of a sequence of points between miles 11 and 15. Wave conditions are rougher in this area, and launching and landing on the steep, cobble-and-boulder beaches between each two gnarled points can be difficult even in moderate weather. Camping is possible in these marginal and rather desolate niches. Some of the cobble beaches are backed by scrub, others by sharp, flaky rockbeds. Seclusion is almost guaranteed.

Between the third and fourth points of the larger Punta Final promontory, a lagoon at mile 15 invites exploration. Sea lions occasionally frolic in this area and in the waters to the south.

There is no way to return from this area except to paddle. The Sierra San Francisquito rises flush against the shore; cutting off all inland access.

And Beyond

The stretch of cliffs from here south extends for 75 miles to Bahía de Los Ángeles, with one respite at the small fish camp of Calamujué (8 miles south) and a few minor camps and communities just north of Bahía de L.A.—some of the toughest and most remote paddling in the Sea of Cortés.

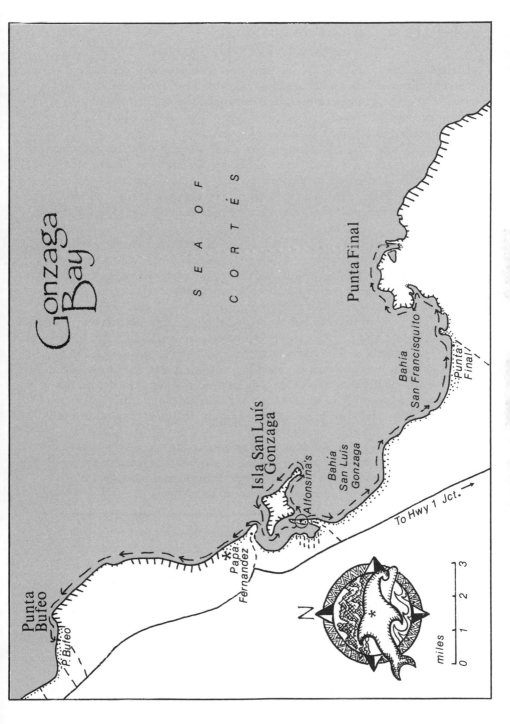

Gonzaga Bay

S E A   O F

C O R T É S

Punta Final

Bahía
San Francisquito

·Punta·
Final/

Isla San Luís
Gonzaga

·Alfonsina's

Bahía
San Luís
Gonzaga

To Hwy 1 Jct.

Papá·
Fernandez

Punta
Bufeo

·P. Bufeo

N

miles

0   1   2   3

ROUTE 8   Bahía de Los Ángeles:
The Poor Man's Galapagos

Trip Summary: An 18.5–20-mile trip around an island-studded bay, offering glimpses into an unparalleled variety of environments, both desert and marine, against a backdrop of rugged mountain scenery.
Trip Length: 2–3 days.
Charts: MEX Topo H12 C42, H12 C52 at 1:50,000
Getting There: From Tijuana to the Bahía de Los Ángeles junction
(well-signed; site of a restaurant and PEMEX) is 364 miles via Highway
1. The side road at this junction is paved, but riddled with potholes.
Follow it 42 miles to Bahía de L.A., being extra cautious at the very end,
when undercarriage-scraping *topes* announce your arrival at the town
proper.
Note: There is no public transport in or out of Bahía de L.A.; hitchhiking
is possible but not common.
Climate & Conditions: Mild in winter, with temperatures in the 50–
60°s; hot in summer with 90–100°+ days and little to no precipitation.
Water surface temperatures range from 61° in January to 72° in July.

Wind is no stranger to Bahía de L.A., though local patterns are still
mysterious to all but the most knowing area fishermen. In short, gales
here can be fierce and unpredictable; the only way to outsmart them is
to stay on land if they start blowing before your departure (sometimes
for 3-day+ spells) and to ask locals about their weather hunches for the
days you'll be out. Also, maximize your chances by paddling early in
the morning, and carrying enough supplies for unanticipated island
layover days.

Generally, wind is from the north or west in the winter (the latter of
these are the strongest winds, funneling down from the mountains west
of town). In summer, wind is gentler but its direction is more variable; it
usually blows from the southeast, south or southwest.

---

*Islands exhibit evolution in action, a natural laboratory for the study of
how species compete and interact in remote, undisturbed settings unrep-
licable on mainlands. Darwin had his Galapagos. We, who can't make it
that far, have the islands of the Cortés. They are more than an adequate
substitute, and perhaps because of their relative closeness, we take them
for granted. In reality they are, in one researcher's words, "The most pristine archipelagoes left on earth."*

*Bahía de Los Ángeles, a large bay midway down Baja's eastern
coast, provides access to 15 of these islands. Most important to the kayaker, most of these are in a tight cluster no more than 4 miles offshore.
No other area in Baja offers the average paddler an opportunity to visit*

*so many isles, each of them unique, without requiring long days of pad-
dling or a sequence of dangerous crossings.*

*En route to the islands one may spot any of over a dozen cetaceans
that frequent this area: among them blue, gray, finback, Bryde's, Minke,
humpback, pilot, sperm, pygmy sperm, killer, and false killer whales; as
well as bottlenose and common dolphins. Sea lions are also commonly
encountered. On the islands themselves, there are over 50 species of
birds and at least 5 species of lizards. In this latter category one finds
the giant chuckwalla, a lizard about 2 feet long, which is able to store
freshwater internally for long periods, as well as desalinate seawater
within its body once the freshwater has been used. When threatened, the
chuckwalla distends its abdomen, anchoring itself between rocks. Most
of the time, however, it can be seen sunning itself out in the open, on the
islands of Ventana, Smith, Piojo and Cabeza de Caballo.*

*The physical aspects of the islands are as diverse as the area's living
inhabitants: within a day's paddle one may see a volcano, a lagoon, a
mangrove swamp, whitened bluffs, rock arches, crushed-shell beaches,
sandy arroyos and cactus-covered slopes.*

*The amateur naturalist would probably run out of freshwater and
food rations before he or she tired of exploring the bay. What separates
Bahía de Los Ángeles from other remote and biologically diverse areas in
Baja, however, is the fact that there are complementary attractions to be
found on land. Make no mistake, the town itself is far from cosmopoli-
tan. Even so it has a valuable museum, the Museo de Naturaleza y Cul-
tura, which has many local bird and marine mammal displays, a large
shell collection, and artifacts from the town's early mining days (open
2–4 p.m. in winter, 3–5 p.m. in summer).*

*American community colleges operate summer classes out of the
Vermilion Sea Field Station, a research facility at the southern end of
Bahía de L.A. (Anyone may register for the classes through Glendale
Community College in California. On a more casual basis, its worth in-
troducing yourself to the staff there if you have specific questions on lo-
cal wildlife.)*

*Finally, a Mexican conservationist, Antonio Resendiz, tends a sea-
turtle facility on the shore north of town. Volunteers help Resendiz care
for several endangered species of sea turtles; though visits are usually
planned through organizations in the U.S., enthusiasts might inquire
locally for a chance to see the facility.*

*These small institutions present many informal opportunities to
combine a kayak trip with local nature study. And of course, with a
camp set upon one of the isles, just about anyone can enjoy playing the
amateur naturalist, or the castaway philosopher, for a few days.*

Starting Point: Bahía de Los Ángeles

The town of Bahía de L.A. grew up around mining and kept growing with an influx of game fishermen and tourists from the north, most of them seeking dorado and yellowtail. Some call it charming, others call it bleak; in any event, it is small and rather dirty but certainly interesting and *ciento por ciento* Baja.

There are three hotels, three trailer parks, four restaurants, at least five minimarts, a beer store, PEMEX (fuel supply unreliable), medical clinic and the aforementioned museum. Everything is easy walking distance from the shore, and the Casa Díaz hotel and Guillermo's Trailer park, both on the main road in town, offer easiest car parking and kayak launch. Guillermo's is also notable for its restaurant, where pink tablecloths, full-course meals and a well-stocked bar start desert-weary visitors salivating. The Díaz restaurant gets decent reviews, though the atmosphere at Casa Díaz is not what most travel guides claim; since the death of Papa Díaz, Bahía de L.A.'s most noted patriarch, nothing is quite as personal as it used to be.

Beach camping is popular north of town near the Punta La Gringa, though at spots one may have to vie with RVs.

The inner part of the bay, fronting the town, is very sheltered and makes for an easy launch. The beach in front of Guillermo's Trailer Park and the Díaz compound (behind the PEMEX) is used by sailboaters, fishermen, and just about everyone else.

Circling the Isles

Launching from the beach, one will paddle past a small flotilla of anchored sailboats and fishing vessels, and then head for 1 mile to Punta Arena, a low-profile point that marks the northern limit of the inner bay and is the site of a red-and-white horizontally striped light tower.

From Punta Arena (literally, "Sand Point") to Punta La Gringa extends a long, sandy beach popular for camping, shelling and loafing. A stretch of shallows, the *Bajo*, fronts this beach for several miles.

After paddling north along the shore for 1–1.5 miles, one is in good position to cross over to the islands. The rugged, earth-toned desert isles may seem difficult to distinguish from afar, so take a moment to orient yourself. Ventana, the largest in the central cluster, is reddish-brown, with two smaller tan-and-white isles directly off its northwest side. This is not to be confused with Cabeza de Caballo, which is farther away, due east, and more darkly colored. Smith (Coronado) Island is the long island to the northeast, easily distinguished by the volcanic cone at its northern extremity. (The enormous island that forms the bay's seaward backdrop is 45-mile Ángel de la Guarda, a veritable mountain range rising from the sea; not shown on this map.)

The crossing to the western shore of Ventana is 2.5 miles (total mile-age to this point: 5 miles). There are two gravel landings on this side of Ventana, the larger and better of these can be located just past a rugged mound of land connected to the isle by a low, flat strip. Just off this point to the northwest are two small, lightly colored, rocky isles: Cerraja and Llave (or Lock and Key).

Proceeding through the channel that runs between Cerraja and Llave on the west and Ventana on the east, one comes to a beautifully sheltered, horseshoe-shaped cove on Ventana's northern side. The cove is ringed by bluffs, flattening out to a level, sand-and-gravel beach at the back of the cove. This beach is one of the three best campsites on the route. Crumbling, rocky slopes behind the beach are good places to spot your first chuckwalla, ospreys reportedly nest on Ventana, and birdcalls echo from the nearby bluffs.

Directly across from the mouth of the cove is the lime-covered Isla Flecha, or Arrow (also known as "Borrego," or "Sheep"). Almost hidden behind it is Isla Jorobado, or "Hunchback." Directly north of the cove are the rocky, tan-colored twin islands of Pata and Bota, "Foot" and "Boot." (These have also been translated as "Duck" and "Bottle.")

A picturesque, sheltered, clearwater channel runs between the two islands, and is a favored anchoring spot for sailboats. Snorkeling and scallop-collecting are popular in the channel. Pata, the northern island, has a crushed-shell beach and is a good camping spot. The foundation of a stone windbreak can be found on the island's eastern end. A short sandy trail winds from this foundation up to a ridge, from which one can view the other side of the inland, and in the distance, the islands Smith and Calavera.

East of Pata and Bota is a long, flat, white-and-tan islet named Rasita (also known as San Aremar). Piojo (or "Louse") Island, a tan, mesa-shaped isle is farther east, and is the site of a pelican colony. (It is ecologically sensitive, as well as very smelly; landing there is discouraged.)

At mile 6, one exits the channel and, rounding Pata, one can see the small white, dome-shaped islet, Isla Calavera, or "Skull" (which looks like precisely that) to the north. Behind it is the largest of the Bahía de Los Ángeles islands, Isla Smith (also known as Coronado), which is 4.5 miles long.

The crossing to Smith is 2 miles long. Currents and wind can be stronger here, aggravated by the long channel formed between Isla Smith and the mainland shore; one is outside the sheltering reaches of the bay's headlands at this point. Passing by Calavera, halfway to Smith, one may hear the loud barking of sea lions, or even catch them snoozing, flippers and nose just above the surface, in the waters en route. There is also a cormorant nesting site on Calavera.

The cry of red-beaked oystercatchers greets kayakers arriving at Isla Smith, at mile 8. Two small inlets are found on Smith's southwest side. The first leads deep into a mangrove swamp. The area is frequently inundated and very buggy, but worth a quick detour to see the many flatfish and rays that blanket the inlet's silt bottom. The second inlet is fairly hidden, but worth the search: inside one finds a mysterious lagoon which winds far enough eastward to almost pinch off the southern part of Smith. By landing on the scrubby dunes at the back of the green lagoon and walking only a few yards, one comes to the island's eastern shore and the clearer blue waters of the open Cortés. At high tide, a reversing waterfall flows over the dune spit.

Camping is possible in this area (being careful for the tides, of course, as well as rattlesnakes) or at several smaller gravel-sand landings farther down Smith's eastern side. Snorkeling is also good here, and at the very southeastern point of Smith, at mile 10, there is a large frigatebird roosting site. The return crossing of 3 miles brings one to the southeastern tip of Ventana, at mile 13. Here one discovers the meaning of the island's name: Ventana, or "Window." A large rock archway forms a natural peephole. There are rocky landing spots before and after the arch. This is a great whalewatching and snorkeling spot.

If winds are strong, one can continue following the southern shore of Ventana, returning to the main shore in just over 3 miles and retracing the route back along Punta Arena and into the inner bay, finishing the route at mile 18.5.

Alternatively, in calm weather, one can paddle in the direction of Isla Cabeza de Caballo ("Horsehead"). A reef is found midway between Ventana and Isla Cabeza de Caballo; the rocky pinnacles are usually visible just above the water. A wreck lies 20 feet from the southeastern pinnacle, in water 10–50 feet deep, according to Walt Peterson in his *Baja Adventure Book*. There is good snorkeling off the northern point of Cabeza de Caballo, as well as good fishing off the western shore. The small Islas Los Gemelitos, or Little Twins, are visible 1 mile south. A 5-mile crossing back to Bahía de Los Ángeles finishes the route at mile 20.

Finish

From sea, the town is best distinguished by looking for the greener vegetation against the mountainous backdrop; this marks the town's center. As one enters the inner bay, the pink buildings with palapas (Guillermo's) and the arched doorways behind and to the left of the stone pier (Díaz property) become visible.

Other Options

Puerto Don Juan is a sheltered bay with a sand beach 8 miles from Bahía de L.A. One of the best natural harbors in the Cortés, it is popular with the yachting crowd.

The trip to Las Ánimas, approximately 15–20 miles south of Bahía de L.A. depending on how closely you hug the shore, is also an option, though shuttling back from the fishing village of Las Ánimas can be difficult.

Pangas can be chartered at Casa Díaz and elsewhere in town for a trip out to Isla Raza, a noted bird sanctuary in the chain of islands that lie off the Canal de Salsipuedes, southeast of Punta Las Ánimas.

High tides happen

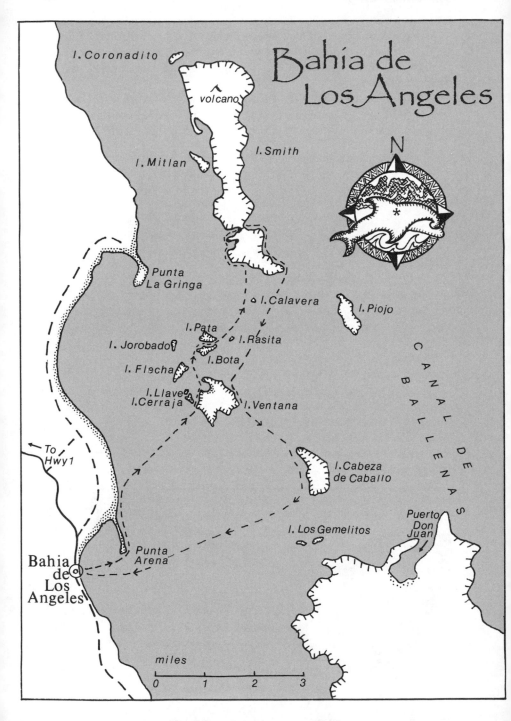

Bahía de Los Angeles

I. Coronadito

volcano

I. Smith

I. Mitlan

N

Punta La Gringa

I. Calavera

I. Piojo

I. Pata

I. Jorobado

I. Rasita

I. Bota

I. Flecha

I. Llave

I. Cerraja

I. Ventana

C A N A L   D E   B A L L E N A S

To Hwy 1

I. Cabeza de Caballo

I. Los Gemelitos

Puerto Don Juan

Punta Arena

Bahía de Los Angeles

miles

0   1   2   3

Chapter 6

The Southern Cortés

ROUTE 9   Santa Rosalía to Punta Chivato: Fisherman's Tour

Trip Summary: A 32-mile trip from the town of Santa Rosalía to the remote resort at Punta Chivato, with excellent fishing and snorkeling along the way. Even if you're not interested in trolling a line, the first hints of the semitropics make for a pleasant paddling and camping trip. An optional sidetrip leads to the island of San Marcos.

Trip Length: 3–5 days.

Charts: MEX Topo G12 A36, G12 A46, G12 A47 at 1:50,000; U.S. Nautical 21161

Getting There: Santa Rosalía is 577 miles south of Tijuana via Highway 1. The highway descends from a steep grade, leveling out and meeting up with the coast just before town. Downtown Santa Rosalía is organized around several main avenues running perpendicular to the highway and the waterfront

Santa Rosalía is on the Highway 1 bus route; the stop is just south of town across from the beach. Hitchhiking in and out is fairly easy (try the PEMEX). A ferry transports visitors to and from mainland Mexico.

The route's finish point, Punta Chivato, is at the end of a 14-mile washboard-surface sideroad signed "Punta Chivato" off of Highway 1. No public transportation is available to or from this remote resort, although you may be able to arrange for a ride back to the highway with a resort guest. A round-trip paddle or a shortened trip, ending at San Bruno (just off Highway 1), may be preferable for those concerned about transportation.

Climate & Conditions: Like the rest of Baja California Sur, Santa Rosalía experiences mild winters, with daytime temperatures in the 60°s, and hot summers of 90°+.

Water surface temperatures in the Cortés range from 62° in January to 75° in July.

Winds are from the northwest from November to May, with particularly strong spells of north winds in winter months, sometimes shifting to easterlies in the afternoon. More gentle and more variable

winds are the norm the rest of the year, usually from the west to southeast. Strong westerly winds can gust at any time. Year-round, winds
pick up in the afternoon.

---

*Like many Baja visitors, I remember reading Ray Cannon's legendary
Sea of Cortez, a collection of fishing tales written at a time when visiting fishermen were a rare and hardy breed. Some of the tales unnerved
me. Treacherous windstorms and bizarre marine phenomena? Feeding
frenzies visible from a mile away, the sea churning with death and de-
struction? Although hardly a fisherman, I was nonetheless enthralled.
This place seemed odd and strange, and like nearly everyone who read
Cannon's book, I wanted to see it for myself.*

*By the time I started paddling Baja, I had become a bit more dubi-
ous. I had met enough fishermen to understand how fish tales come into
being . . . hot sun, mirages, a little beer, a little bravado. Sure, I believed
that Baja was a fisherman's paradise; but feeding frenzies? Churning
water? Fish jumping after every line?*

*My partner and I had suffered miserable luck with our own fishing.
Even though we had brought an immense tackle box stuffed with every
kind of lure, and a fancy rod and reel, we hadn't landed enough fish for
one decent meal. Our luck turned even more sour when we lost most of
our gear in Santa Rosalía. Left with only a spoon or two and some
heavy line, I gave up on any ceviche or huachinango feasts.*

*Brian resorted to stoically towing a basic line from the back of his
kayak. He tended this simple, sorry line from Santa Rosalía to San Lucas. A few nibbles encouraged him along the way. Just past San Lucas,
we saw our first palm tree. Vegetation along the coast, and the warmest
waters we'd felt all trip contributed to a tropical ambience. More nibbles
began to strike Brian's simple line than any of the fancier contraptions
he'd rigged earlier in our trip, when he'd had more and better gear.*

*Late the following day, paddling the channel between Isla San Mar-
cos and the main shore, we saw a strange thing. The sunlight striking
the water ahead seemed to make it shimmer and dance. We glimpsed silver shades glittering on the surface, which had become more roughly
textured even though no winds blew.*

*Squinting, we paddled ahead toward the agitated patch of water,
which was now in full boil. A few large fish flew into the air ahead of
our crafts. Even before we had caught up with the bubbling silver water,
Brian's line responded to a strike. He pulled up a roosterfish. As soon as
his line was trailing behind the kayak again, he pulled up another.*

*The feeding frenzy continued around us, with fish of all sizes flop-
ping and flying, escaping from or pursuing other fish. The spectacle was
more curious than frightening. Cannon's description of a boiling sea
may have been slightly exaggerated, but only slightly.*

We survived the mayhem and paddled toward the fishing resort of Punta Chivato, with fish ready to grill as soon as we made landfall, and a few fish tales of our own to swap at the hotel bar. As for the simple contraption Brian rigged for his kayak, he hasn't fished any other way since.

Starting Point: Santa Rosalía

Founded by the French-owned El Boleo Copper Company, Santa Rosalía grew into a small but sophisticated outpost with clapboard houses, a church built by Alexandre Gustave Eiffel, and narrow, tree-lined streets. The French pulled out of the mine in the '50s, but left their French-style bakery behind (of special interest to any travelers burned out on tortillas). Other French accents remain as well: residents dress with an unusual flair; and every occupation and every social group, from schoolgirls to the police (of which there are three or four kinds) has its own spiffy uniform.

Restaurants and hotels are numerous, grocery stores are surprisingly well-stocked, and a number of specialty stores offer everything from candy and comics to fishing gear and household wares. Not bad for a town of 14,000.

The Mahatma Gandhi library has interesting local historical documents worth perusing on a hot or a windy day. The cantinas near the foothills on the west side of town offer nighttime diversions for the curious and the brave.

There are no campgrounds in town. The Santa Rosalía marina is a potential storage place for your kayak if you're planning on hanging around for a few days. The beach just south of the marina and ferry is smelly, rocky and not very attractive, but adequate for launching or minimal camping.

Launching from the beach, one paddles past several rocky beaches backed by low bluffs. The first landmark appears at mile 1.5 where a small offshore rock supports a light tower. Just past this rock is the month of an estuary, the Estero San Luciano, which can be easily missed from the cockpit of a kayak. If the estuary is flooded, you can paddle it 0.5 mile inland, arriving at an RV park/campground.

Proceeding past the estuary's mouth, the coastal scenery becomes more interesting. The Morro El Fraile ("Friar's Knoll") is visible at mile 3.0. Sandstone bluffs set flush against the shore form sculpted overhangs. In one spot, a smooth, flat ledge provides a perfect sheltered tent site.

Snorkeling off the rocky beaches fronting the bluffs is excellent, with virtual forests of seaweed providing hiding places for the colorful fish that become increasingly diverse and abundant as you move south. You may come face-to-face with eels anchored in the rocks.

Children from Santa Rosalía brief us on the relative merits of sharks and dolphins

Punta Gorda, the last point on the range of bluffs lining the shore, is at mile 5.0. The coast flattens out for the next few miles until a tall mound on the shore, known locally as "The Haystack," provides a good landmark near mile 7.5. Fishermen from San Lucas frequently motor up to the waters off this point; they claim the fishing is excellent here.

The Barra San Lucas, a thin, dune-covered sandbar, extends for 3 miles past the haystack, sheltering the Caleta San Lucas behind it. At mile 10.5, at the end of the bar, lies the entrance to the Caleta San Lucas and the small RV park and community of San Lucas that sits nestled at the back of the cove.

Continuing south from the end of the bar, past the cove's entrance to the main shore, you paddle through 0.5 mile of white-sand shallows. If you ever wanted to observe stingrays up close, this is the place; they literally blanket the sandy floor here. A wreck is also reported in this area.

A sand beach and stand of palm trees is at mile 11.0, the first tropical campsite you'll see this far north on the Cortés. Thick vegetation attracts a few bugs, but also provides welcome shade.

The RV park and fishing community of San Bruno extend from mile 14.5 to mile 15.0. Attractive beaches provide good tent sites in this area.

Water is available. If you're desperate for a restaurant meal, you can land at San Bruno, walk inland to Highway 1, and turn left. The trek to "La Peninsular," owned by an American-Mexican couple, is just over 1 mile.

(San Bruno is also a good point from which to depart for a paddle to Isla San Marcos, described at the end of this route.)

After several small, rocky points, an attractive sand beach is located at mile 18.5. Marginal sand-and-gravel beaches backed by low bluffs appear at intervals for the next several miles. A prominent point is at mile 21. The shallowness of the channel between the main shore and Isla San Marcos contributes to the speed with which waters are whipped up in this area, particularly when an afternoon wind blows from the east.

At mile 22, an estuary, the Estero San Marcos, is visible when flooded. A few shade trees just past the rocky beach provide a good lunch or camping spot. People have been observed digging in the estuary when it's dry—for clams, buried treasure or something more mysterious, I'm not sure.

High bluffs hug the shore from mile 24.5 to 27. A stretch of sandy beach is the last semiprivate camping spot, between miles 27 and 27.5. If you're hoping for a final dose of solitude before paddling into range of the resort, this may be it.

The point supporting a light tower (at last check, not in operation) at mile 29 is literally Punta Chivato, or "Chivato Point," but not the Punta Chivato *resort*. The sequence of points that form the headland of this knob of land may seem endless if you're expecting the hotel to come into view. You still have a few more miles to paddle.

A prominent patch of light-colored sand dunes marks the area between the tiny unnamed point at mile 30 and the larger Punta Cerotito at mile 31. RVs come into view on the sandy beach campground between Punta Cerotito and the T-shaped point, Punta Santa Inés (also known as Punta Cacarizo). There are several good snorkeling and fishing spots in this area; ask fellow anglers and campers about what's biting.

Several red-roofed private houses set high upon the bluffs are visible past Punta Santa Inés. The Hotel Punta Chivato is just before mile 32. The most convenient landing area is a sandy beach dotted with shade palapas just past the bluffs, with stairs winding up to the resort.

Finish: Punta Chivato

Punta Chivato is a fly-in and RV resort catering primarily to game fishermen. The hotel has a pool, restaurant, bar, and gift shop with fishing tackle. The restaurant will cook any fish you catch, and pangas and guides can be hired for serious fishing outings through the hotel.

Camping facilities are available for a fee; if you want to camp free and away from the crowds, land before you round Chivato Point or continue past the resort to the western shore of Bahía Santa Inés. To restock basic supplies, go to the small Conasupo grocery store on the road behind the resort.

Other Options

Isla San Marcos, site of an active gypsum mine, a small village and several remote camping beaches, offers a tempting sidetrip from this route. From the camp of San Bruno to the village on the island's southwest corner is a paddle of 5 miles. A shorter crossing, from the main shore directly south of the island to the island's southernmost tip is a paddle of 3 miles. The island itself has a perimeter of nearly 15 miles. Clearly, exploring Isla San Marcos could keep a paddler occupied for 3–4 days, and deserves a route unto itself.

Since I've never paddled there, however, I'll have to limit any description to the comments passed on by Dan Breedon, a kayaker who lives in San Bruno and occasionally paddles to Isla San Marcos alone or with friends to camp and spearfish.

Paddling the island clockwise from the village, Dan describes the western side of the island as primarily rocky coastline. If the northerly winds are blowing, there are a couple of protected coves on the western side of the island just south of Punta Piedra Blanca, near an abandoned fish camp. The northwestern end of the island has several beautiful camping spots with sandy or pebble beaches with good fishing. At the very northern tip of the island there are several nice camping spots, although they may be difficult to enter if northerlies are strong.

On the northeast side of the island, there are about four good beaches. Along the remainder of the east side, the coast is primarily rocky, with a few small coves suitable for landing. On the south side of the island, the Bahía Puerto Viejo is backed by a broad, sandy beach although there aren't many fish there. The Roca Lobos, a small offshore rock south of Bahía Puerto Viejo, is not suitable for camping, but permits landing and has excellent snorkeling.

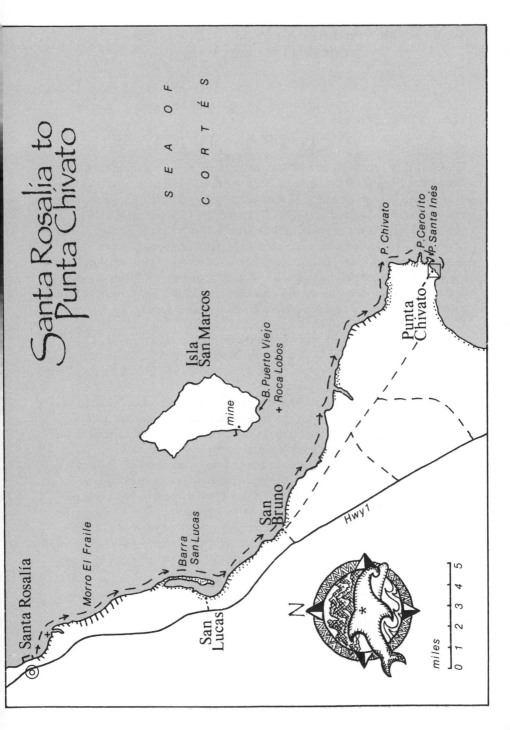

Santa Rosalía to Punta Chivato

SEA OF CORTÉS

Isla San Marcos

mine

B. Puerto Viejo
+ Roca Lobos

P. Chivato
P. Cerolito
P. Santa Inés

Punta Chivato

San Bruno

Hwy 1

Barra San Lucas

Morro El Fraile

Santa Rosalía

San Lucas

N

miles
0 1 2 3 4 5

ROUTE 10   Around Mulegé: 3 Day-Trips from the Tropical Village

Trip Summary: Mulegé provides the base camp for three short trips: a lazy paddle along the Río Mulegé, a 15-mile jaunt north to Punta Chivato, and an equally challenging 14-mile paddle south to the beach camp of Playa Santispac.

Trip Length: 1 day per trip. (North & south trips can be extended to 2 days with camping en route.)

Charts: MEX Topos at 1:50,000. Inconveniently, this small area is right at the intersection of several charts. For the fullest Mexican topo coverage, you'll need MEX G12 A46, G12 A47, G12 A56, and G12 A57. (75% of the relevant area is covered on G12 A57, however.) U.S. Nautical 21161

Getting There: Mulegé is 615 miles south of Tijuana via Highway 1. The town itself is 2 miles inland, on the north bank of a small "river" (actually an estuary), the Río Mulegé. The main street, Francisco Madero, runs northeast and turns into a narrow dirt road that follows the estuary for 2 miles to the sea. At the end of this road is a lighthouse poised atop El Sombrerito, a hat-shaped hill, and a wide beach facing the open Cortés.

Mulegé is on the Highway 1 bus route; the stop is just west of town. Hitchhiking in and out is fairly easy. From Mulegé to the beach is a pleasant 2-mile walk; or you can easily flag someone down for a ride. To grab a taxi, go to the town square.

Climate & Conditions: Like the rest of Baja California Sur, Mulegé experiences mild winters, with daytime temperatures averaging 60–70°, and hot summers of 90°+. The main difference is that the summers are very muggy, even stifling as compared to drier areas in Baja

Water surface temperatures in the Cortés range from 62° in January to 75° in July (warmer temperatures within Bahía Concepción).

Winds are from the northwest from November to May, with particularly strong spells of north winds in winter months. More gentle and more variable winds are the norm the rest of the year, usually from the southwest to southeast. Year-round, winds pick up in the afternoon.

The Río Mulegé is sheltered enough to permit paddling at all times of day (and night).

With thatched hut palapas, an estuary flanked by winding dirt roads and thick stands of date palms, Mulegé is the ultimate Baja oasis. Though far north of the Tropic of Cancer, the small town is nonetheless endowed with a sultry, tropical ambience, which has long attracted tourists. Too many tourists? Perhaps. But Mulegé is still very small, and manages to retain a character of its own, with little immediate danger of becoming either a San Felipe or a Cabo San Lucas.

Every time I've come to Mulegé, I've stayed longer than I'd planned. The pace of life here is slow, the river invites evening strolls along its banks, and a handful of fairly good restaurants and beachfront stands keep one well-fed and content. Especially in summer, when humid days and warm, breezy evenings dull and pacify the senses, there is little motivation to do anything rash, like embark on an overly long or difficult journey. Instead, a 2–4 mile paddle up and down the river, preferably at sunset, seems like more than enough of a workout. If that proves too tiring, one can simply float.

Of course, if you are intent on being active, there are two more challenging trips north and south of the estuary's entrance. Both end at beaches, the one to the north being superior for shelling and fishing, the one to the south perfectly suited for more bikini-oriented activities: swimming, lying around, waiting for tamale vendors to amble by.

Whether or not an evening river paddle or a night-time beach stroll makes you feel tropically somnambulistic, you may be convinced you are dreaming. The reason: a bizarre and startling phenomenon, particularly common to these parts in midsummer. Stamping one's feet on the damp sand elicits sparklike flashes. A fish darting close to the surface appears like a stream of light. Any moving creature, emerging from the depths, glows. The seasonal display, called bioluminescence, is caused by an abundance of dinoflagellates, a microscopic, unicellular species of phytoplankton, which light up whenever the surrounding water is disturbed.

Paddling is the perfect way to see Mulegé's environs: as a way of travel that is unjarring, rhythmic, and hopefully not too fast; on a sea that glistens at dawn, pounds the shore in late afternoon, and glows at night. There is not as much isolation here as on other routes, but the people one encounters are generally friendly and sedate. There is not much to do, but no one seems to mind.

Starting Point: Mulegé and Mulegé Beach

The town is organized around a handful of roads that converge at a square. A post office, several hotels and restaurants and small grocery store are all nearby. There are also accommodations at the numerous RV parks on the south bank of the river, reached by Highway 1 south of Mulegé, as well as the posh Hotel Serenidad, owned by the local American consul. Of particular interest in town is Mulegé Divers, a shop operated by Miguel and Claudia Quintana at 45 Calle Madero. The dive shop offers trips and equipment, and is a good place to ask for informal info about the area.

Also worth exploring by foot are Mulegé's historic mission and its penitentiary, the latter of which was famous because its prisoners were released each morning and called back, at the blow of a conch shell, for lockup each evening.

The beach at the end of the estuary is the best base from which to kayak the area. At one end of the beach, a small seaside restaurant serves seafood cocktails as well as the regular alcoholic variety; an outhouse is behind the restaurant.

Farther down the beach, several thatched palapa frames provide shade (watch out for scorpions in the corners), and a small fee may be collected for camping and parking there.

A man named Miguel and his family run the lighthouse next to the beach, on top of the hill El Sombrerito, or "Little Hat." Miguel doesn't speak English, but with a little Spanish you may be able to arrange to leave your car parked next to the lighthouse while you paddle north or south. A second option is to park in town, and walk or hitchhike the 2 miles to the beach. Stairs leading up to the top of El Sombrerito enable you to get a better view of the area.

Trip 1: Río Mulegé

A paddle up the Río Mulegé requires few instructions or warnings. It is a sightseeing paddle, a sunset or moonlight paddle, and a good place to learn basic skills or to get accustomed to a new kayak before heading to other routes.

The Río Mulegé, also called the Río Rosalía, is actually a saltwater estuary, not a river, although a small trickle of freshwater does enter it before the overpass near town. Great floods generated by *chubascos* swelled the estuary and nearly wiped out the town in 1770 and again in 1959. A different kind of deluge occurred at the estuary's mouth in 1847, when the U.S. Navy invaded and occupied Mulegé during the Mexican-American War.

Launching next to the sailboats and pangas moored by the lighthouse, you begin paddling up the estuary. Thick stands of mangroves immediately divide the river into two ribbonlike passages. The southern of these has a more developed, almost suburban shore. Beyond a boat launch is the Hotel Serenidad. About ½ mile farther up the estuary are three RV parks. Numerous ranch-style houses have been built along the shore with small piers and boats moored in front; most of these are owned or rented by Americans. A curious sight on the 4th of July is the incredible number of barbecues and lawn parties held on the banks of this unusual Mexican "river"; obviously, the invasion that took place in 1847 has in many ways continued into the present.

A few of these residents own kayaks. You may encounter someone like Esther, an American woman who can be seen paddling steadily to El Sombrerito and back in her open-top just as dusk is falling.

The mangroves break up and peter out as the estuary narrows. Great blue herons stand among the gnarled roots, squawking like cranky pterodactyls and flapping to the far bank when a stealthy kayaker gets too close.

The date palms, dusty lanes and tropical ambience of Mulegé now seem pleasantly exotic, but this same environment once provided a breeding ground for the anopheles mosquito, the carrier of malaria. Even after the disease was eradicated, the reputation remained. In *The Log from the Sea of Cortez* Steinbeck jokes about deciding to pass up Mulegé, due in part to its malarial reputation and even more to avoid its port fees, but then looks back with regret. "We passed up Mulegé . . . and it looked gay against the mountains, red-roofed and white-walled."

Just over 2 miles from the lighthouse, the estuary narrows even more and gets mucky, and the tangle of vegetation chokes any further passage. Overhead, one can see the bridge over which Highway 1 continues south. Considering the number of local postcards that proudly boast pictures of this bridge, one gets the idea that it is a source of civic pride. Landing in the brush on the north bank, one can meander through a few back yards and walk to the square for ice cream or a taco, or turn around and paddle back to the beach.

Trip 2: North to Punta Chivato

This route provides moderately challenging paddling with opportunities for fishing and isolated camping. Fine-sand beaches extend for much of the second half of the route. The area can be windy, but stopping points are plentiful and, with adequate supplies, delays can be welcome. A resort provides hotel rooms, restaurant and camping facilities at trip's end, but one warning: a return paddle may be the easiest way back to Mulegé, since there is absolutely no public transport back to the main highway.

Launching at El Sombrerito, one heads north toward the first point, Cerro El Mirasol, a large hill on the shore. Beyond this is a larger point at mile 1, Punta Prieta. Punta Prieta, or Rocky Point, has a thumblike appendage.

Beyond this point is a fairly sheltered aquamarine bay, framed by low bluffs. Proceeding along the coast, the next points are Punta Colorada just past mile 2, and Punta Raza at mile 3.

Around these rocky areas I've often been startled by the sudden apparition of black or neon tubes protruding from the water, and here stopped myself just in time to keep from running over the snorkelers floating beneath them. Mexican snorkelers rarely look up, and their still, barely submerged bodies look eerily lifeless. Considering the large number of snorkelers in this area, there must be a good supply of shellfish; you may want to stop and strap on fins yourself.

The coastline for the middle section of the route, approximately miles 3 to 7, is composed of low hills sloping down to pebble beaches, with large rocky areas just offshore exposed at low tide. Fishing is good here. My partner has pulled in several prize catches, including rooster-fish, surprisingly close to shore.

Miles 7 to 12, the central part of the wide, unsheltered Bahía Santa Inés, feature a stretch of sandy shore that makes for great camping and beachcombing. To the northeast, three small, flat, featureless islets, the Islas Santa Inés, are visible.

From miles 12 to 14, the exceptional fine-sand beach of Playa La Palmita is noted for its abundance and variety of shells. At the far end of this beach are interesting sandstone ledges. To the north is the large bluffy headland that forms Bahía Santa Inés's northern boundary. Wind blows briskly around these points, and dumping surf can make beach landings tricky.

RVs, boat launches and moored boats, and farther inland an air strip, share the shore from miles 14 to 15. Camping facilities are available here for a fee. The resort of Punta Chivato overlooks the bluffs at mile 15. Past Punta Santa Inés, the T-shaped point just past the resort, there is additional camping space.

Finish: Punta Chivato is a fly-in and RV resort catering primarily to gamefishermen. It is connected to the highway by a 12-mile washboard road. It may be possible to arrange a ride out with a hotel guest, but in general hitchhiking is not as easy here as on better-traveled routes, and there is no public transportation. If you want to restock supplies and paddle back to Mulegé, you will find a Conasupo, or rural grocery store, on the road behind the resort's parking lot.

Trip 3: South to Playa Santispac

This route provides moderately challenging paddling, eased by the consistency of landmarks and landing spots, most of them sand and gravel, all along the way. Highway 1 runs 1–2 miles inland, not merging again with the shore until Playa Santispac; hence, one can easily find some solitude en route, on stretches of shore unreachable by road. Squadrons of pelicans and dolphins are frequently sighted.

Launching at El Sombrerito, one crosses the mouth of the estuary and proceeds south. The shore is sand and gravel, backed by shrubs. Reddish hills form a distant backdrop.

At mile 3.0, Isla El Gallo ("The Rooster"), a level islet almost connected to the shore, acts as an easily sighted landmark. A small lattice-work light tower is perched on the islet. Punta Gallito rises as a prominent hill just opposite Isla El Gallo.

A poolside view of Bahía Santa Inés from the resort
at Punta Chivato

Small shacks are visible in a cove just after Isla El Gallo, followed by
a second sheer-faced hill. The coast is dominated by short bluffs from
here south.

A scrub-and-cactus-dotted valley is visible at mile 4.5, followed by
a large hill, the Cerro El Tiburón, which supports the Estación Micron-
ades Tiburón, or "Shark Microwave Station," a radio tower, at mile 5.0.

From here on, you are entering Bahía Concepción. To the east, Peninsula Concepción forms the rugged headland of Baja's largest bay.
Along the length of the peninsular headland runs the Sierra Los Gav-
ilantes, a range of red rock and pastel-ribboned peaks that provide a
stunning backdrop for the bay's brilliant blue waters.

Looking at a map, one might expect Bahía Concepción to be sheltered by this range, creating a placid inner bay. Instead, the range and
the mainland shore act like a funnel, intensifying wind from the north.
I know of at least two people who have capsized here: the first was an
absolute beginner, the second a seasoned kayaker. Afternoon winds

spring up suddenly, and winter winds can be especially fierce; use caution.

Farther along the coast, the Cerro Los Machos is a triangular rocky point at mile 6.5. Punta San Pedro, at mile 8, is a small RV camp of 7–10 palapas and rotundas. The beach is rock and gravel; the waters offshore are very shallow.

At mile 10 the Cerro Magdalena, a giant, sheer-faced hill, protrudes between two arroyos. This area of sandstone bluffs, ledges, minor sea-caves and interesting formations makes for a good temporary haul-out. A few small niches and overhangs provide rare shade.

Between Punta Arena at mile 10 and the small camp of Playas Punta Arena, where the coast angles southwest, is a constantly changing area of shifting sand and shallows.

The coast rises to form the rocky point of Punta Piedrita, just past mile 13. Rounding this point, one enters Coyote Bay, an island-studded, popular bay at the heart of Bahía Concepción. A series of developed beaches, camps and settlements ring Coyote Bay. The first of these is Playa Santispac, reached at mile 14.

Finish: Playa Santispac is rimmed by fine white sands and bordered by turquoise waters. Palapa huts on shore are used as vacation homes by some, permanent abodes by others. A restaurant-bakery called Anna's provides refreshment for a steady stream of off-highway visitors, as well as water and a limited variety of canned goods. Sailboats and windsurfers cruise around Coyote Bay, and a kayak concession operates out of one of the palapas.

For those who'd like to stay awhile, camping is possible for a fee. Playa Santispac is directly off Highway 1, making for a quick return to Mulegé. Hitchhiking is the transport of choice between the two points; you may be able to arrange a ride personally at Anna's or on the beach.

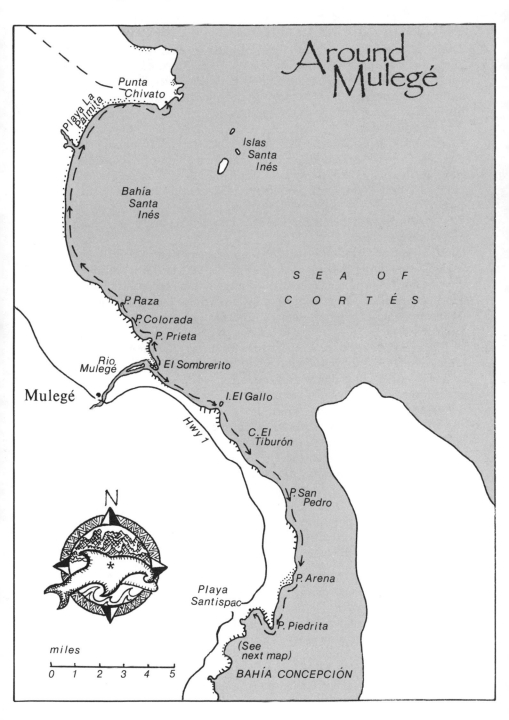

Around
Mulegé

Punta
Chivato

Playa La
Palmita

Islas
Santa
Inés

Bahía
Santa
Inés

S E A   O F

C O R T É S

P. Raza

P. Colorada

P. Prieta

Rio
Mulegé   El Sombrerito

Mulegé   I. El Gallo

Hwy 1

C. El
Tiburón

N

P. San
Pedro

P. Arena

Playa
Santispac

P. Piedrita

miles

(See
next map)

0   1   2   3   4   5

BAHÍA CONCEPCIÓN

ROUTE 11   Bahía Concepción: Island-Cruising

Trip Summary: An approximately 5.5-mile exploration of the small islands and beautiful aquamarine waters off of Playa Santispac, at the
heart of Bahía Concepción. Sheltered paddling, excellent snorkeling,
and opportunities for birdwatching and plant identification are fea-
tured, all within the range of the beginner.

Trip Length: 1 day.

Charts: MEX Topo G12 A57, G12 A67 at 1:50,000; U.S. Nautical 21161

Getting There: Playa Santispac is the first of a chain of Bahía Concepción beaches just off Highway 1, 13.2 miles south of Mulegé. The words
"Playa Santispac" are spelled out in white stones on a hill just before the
turnoff.

The Highway 1 bus runs past Playa Santispac, and hitchhiking in
and out is fairly easy.

Climate & Conditions: Generally, the area experiences mild winters,
with daytime temperatures averaging in the 60°s and hot summers of
90°+. Summers can be humid and stifling when a breeze isn't blowing,
and many residents use this time to head north for their own vacations.
At the same time, there are fewer tourists at summer's peak, a worthwhile tradeoff.

Official water surface temperatures for this region range from 62° in
January to 70° in July, but the inner bays and shallow regions definitely
soar above that latter figure. In Coyote Bay, summer temperatures can
get as high as 90°. When the water gets nearly as warm as human body
temperature, it ceases to be refreshing.

Winds are from the northwest from November to May, with particularly strong spells of north winds in winter months. More gentle
and variable winds are the norm the rest of the year. Although the inner
part of the bay is sheltered, afternoon winds can pick up suddenly and
surprise even the seasoned kayaker.

Note: Each island goes by several names; the most common alternates
have been listed in parentheses. Also, the inner part of Bahía Concepción is often called Coyote Bay. However, Coyote Bay can also refer
more specifically to the waters fronting Coyote Beach, to the south.

---

*I'd paddled a good portion of Baja's coast. I'd been dumped, bumped,
stranded and rescued. I'd interrogated others on their long-distance
strategies, and had defended my own mileage capabilities against the
double-digit feats of more masochistic expeditioners.*

*And then, for fun, I joined a tour to paddle Bahía Concepción. Un-
der the guidance of Becky Aparicio and Roy Mahoff of Baja Tropicales, I
prepared for what I expected to be a rather anticlimactic 5 miles. After
all, this was beginners' stuff, right?*

True enough, during our trip we experienced no surf, no wicked currents, not even any discomfort; instead, only the gentlest of paddling, within the confines of one small, incomparably beautiful bay. And I loved it.

As kayakers who live, work and paddle around Coyote Bay, Roy and Becky have become experts on their immediate environment, and advocates of the kayak as a means to explore it. Slowly circumnavigating the tiny volcanic isle of San Ramón, they talked about the former nesting sites of boobies and pelicans, species whose numbers have taken a dive due to egg-harvesting. Pointing to a cardon cactus, Becky commented on how the fluted ridges of the cacti expand and contract with the availability of water. Around the next point, she predicted an elephant tree: and there it was, rooted in a cleft of the rocky isle's summit; a twisted, stumpy, white-barked monstrosity of a plant. And all this within a few hundred yards.

We didn't make much distance, in fact we often paddled in circles. But we did see the islands and the waters just offshore in a way that the beachbound and the yachtbound can't: up close, from every angle and perspective. When even the kayaks became limiting, we could easily slip off and into the water; the sheltered nature of the bay makes off-kayak snorkeling easy. We gathered clams and headed back to the basecamp for dinner.

This is not meant to be simply a plug for Roy and Becky's tours (after all, you can tour the bay independently), but a plug for a way of touring. The proximity of the isles, which are spaced no more than 0.5 mile apart, encourage intimate exploration. There is no need for bicep-busting mileage, only steady paddling and an attentive eye. The beginner will find his or her first effort rewarded; the expeditioner may unexpectedly become a convert to this kinder, gentler way of kayaking Baja. If I could recommend only one short trip in all of Baja to lure someone into (or back to) the sport, this would be it.

Starting Point: Playa Santispac

The name "Santispac" seems unusual for the Spanish language. One clue to its possibly original spelling comes from a reference in an old cruising guide to a place called San Tispaque.

Playa Santispac is rimmed by fine white sands and bordered by turquoise waters. Palapa huts on shore are used as vacation homes by some, permanent abodes by others. A restaurant-bakery called Anna's provides refreshment for a steady stream of off-highway visitors, and also carries limited canned goods. Not to be depended on, but worth a peek, is the chart of Coyote Bay on the wall of the restaurant; copies may be available for purchase. Sailboats and windsurfers cruise around the bay, and Baja Tropicales operates out of the Palapa Kayaka #17. Camping is possible for a fee. Avoid major holidays, like Spring Break and Christmas Break, when crowds throng.

The islands off of Playa Santispac are volcanic in origin. Few are good for camping or even landing (exceptions noted). The small isles appear like turned-over coconut halves: dark, roughly textured and mound-shaped. The innermost four islands are almost evenly spaced, like the four corners of a square. In the center of this square is a reef. Touring direction is not important; the order presented below is just a suggestion.

Launching from Playa Santispac, the first island is 0.5 mile from shore and is called Isla San Ramón (or Isla Pelicano). There are no spots to land. Boobies and pelicans may be spotted on the island. Cardon, cholla and pitahaya cacti, as well as elephant trees, are also visible. The pitahaya cactus is rather notorious in Baja because the harvesting of its fruit by local indians was once paired with ritualistic orgies. Early missionaries who witnessed this behavior were not amused.

About 0.5 mile southeast of Isla San Ramón is a reef. Snorkeling in this area is excellent, especially with the pursuit of butter clams in mind. Large *hachas* (axes, in English; they are named for their wedge shape) are difficult to pry up from the sand floor but yield a delicious scallop-like meat. The numerous discarded *hacha* shells are becoming a problem in the bay.

About 0.5 mile east-northeast of the reef is Isla Luz (or Isla Pitahaya, or Isla Sin Nombre). Curiously, Sin Nombre means "without a name," a rather inappropriate moniker for an island that currently has three names. A latticework light tower stands atop the island.

This island is just outside the sheltering influence of Punta Piedrita, to the north, so use caution in windy conditions. Isla Luz has a beautiful white-sand beach on its western side—good for stopping but not camping, since it is covered by the high tide. Multicolored fish are abundant around this isle, as are hidden rock niches and corridors worth exploring just under the water's surface. In the vicinity of all the islands, dolphins are commonly spotted.

Just southeast of Isla Luz is the wreck of an old shrimp trawler, close enough to the surface to be explored without scuba equipment. If winds are blowing, the waters will get whipped up and sand may obscure the wreck.

Isla Blanca (or Isla Cueva), just over 0.5 mile south-southwest from Isla Luz, is white and has no landing spots. The warning mentioned for Isla Luz applies here as well; if you're a beginner and it's windy, you might skip this isle.

Completing the square, Isla Coyote (or Isla Liebre) is about 0.75 mile west-northwest from Isla Blanca. It has a small beach on its southwest side, good for landing but not camping.

From Isla Coyote one paddles past rocky Punta Tordilla ("Dapple-gray Point") and into the cove fronting the camp of Posada Concepción. An RV park is on shore; houses are perched on the hills overlooking the cove. A more secluded beach is just around a small point north of Posada Concepción. A hotspring, difficult to locate, dribbles scalding water out of a cluster of rocks on one side of this beach.

You return to Playa Santispac at approximately mile 5.5.

Kayaks on the shore at Playa Santispac

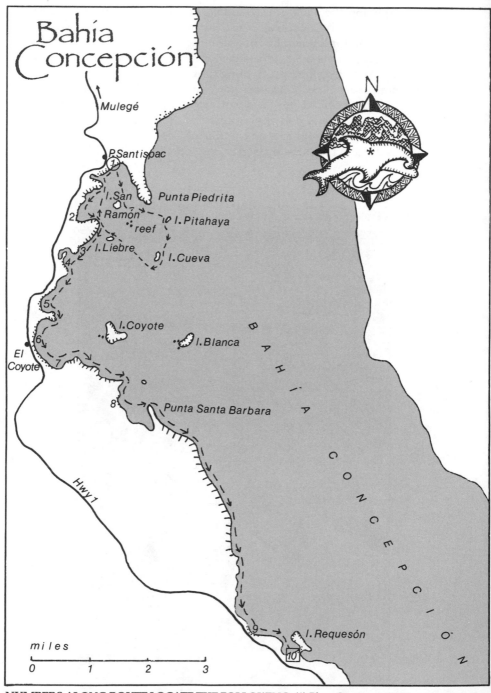

NUMBERS ALONG ROUTE LOCATE THE FOLLOWING: (1) Playa Santispac, (2) Playa Concepción, (3) Playa Escondido, (4) Playa Los Cocos, (5) Playa Burro, (6) Playa Coyote, (7) Playa (Pública) Coyote, (8) Playa Santa Barbara, (9) Playa San Buena Ventura, (10) Playa Requesón

ROUTE 12 Bahía Concepción: Beach-Hopping

Trip Summary: A 12.5-mile beach-hopping tour along the developed western shore of beautiful Bahía Concepción.

Trip Length: 1 day.

Charts: MEX Topo G12 A57, G12 A67 at 1:50,000; U.S. Nautical 21161

Getting There: Playa Santispac is the first of a chain of Bahía Concepción beaches just off Highway 1, 13.2 miles south of Mulegé. The words "Playa Santispac" are spelled out in white stones on a hill just before the turnoff.

The Highway 1 bus runs past Playa Santispac, and hitchhiking in and out is fairly easy.

Climate & Conditions: Generally, the area experiences mild winters, with daytime temperatures averaging in the 60°s and hot summers of 90°+. Summers can be humid and stifling when a breeze isn't blowing, and many residents use this time to head north for their own vacations. At the same time, there are fewer tourists at summer's peak; a worthwhile tradeoff.

Official water surface temperatures for this region range from 62° in January to 75° in July, but the inner bays and shallow regions definitely soar above that latter figure. In Coyote Bay, summer temperatures can get as high as 90°. When the water gets nearly as warm as human body temperature, it ceases to be refreshing.

Winds are from the northwest from November to May, with particularly strong spells of north winds in winter months. More gentle and variable winds are the norm the rest of the year. During the second half of this route you will be in a less sheltered area of the bay which is more open to winds, which can pick up suddenly in the afternoon.

Note: Some of these beaches are under development and descriptions may rapidly become out-of-date.

Kayakers are supposed to love water. This route is about sand. Not just any sand, but some of the finest in Baja: fine and white, or coarse yellow and backed by lush mangroves, or golden and sprinkled with opalescent shell fragments. The kayak, in this case, is a means to an end. By paddling around successive points, you have the best access to all of Bahía Concepción's beaches; you can hold out for your favorite, or visit each one, simply by pulling up and tumbling out of your cockpit onto the sun-drenched shore.

Landing and launching are easy, since most of the area is quite sheltered and there are only the most gently lapping waves where land meets sea. Every cove is unique, with its own shade of water: turquoise, cerulean, aquamarine, emerald.

There are ten small beaches in this particular stretch. Though the entire area is popular among tourists, some beaches are more "discovered" than others. Highway 1 runs along Bahía Concepción, but access by road is harder in some places than others; where the turnoffs are steepest, rockiest or gated off entirely, the kayaker has a definite advantage. A few of the beaches are developed, but development in this case doesn't mean condos and high-rise hotels. At the most, there are spots for RVs, public-use palapa huts for shade, or maybe just a trash can. Acapulco this is not, although during holiday seasons some areas do get crowded, by Baja standards. Camping is possible on most of the beaches. If someone comes by to collect, the fee usually runs $2–5.

Offshore, sailboats outnumber motorboats. Beyond the fluttering masts, one glimpses rocky, volcanic islets: San Ramón, Luz, Coyote, Blanca, Bargo and Guapa. Paddling along the western shore, there are always surprises: tropical fish darting around the rocky points, a dolphin skimming past on its way to some unknown destination, cormorants balancing on offshore rocks, their extended wings pointing the way to the next beach.

Starting Point: Playa Santispac

Playa Santispac is the first beach and one of the most popular. Palapa huts on shore are used as vacation homes by some, permanent abodes by others. A restaurant-bakery called Anna's provides refreshment for a steady stream of off-highway visitors, and also carries limited canned goods. Sailboats and windsurfers cruise around the bay, and Baja Tropicales operates out of the Palapa Kayaka #17.

Launching at Santispac, one paddles west along the rim of developed beachfront. The closest of the offshore islets is Isla San Ramón (or Isla Pelicano), an islet with an abundance of plant and birdlife but no spots for landing.

A short section of steep, rocky shore divides Santispac from the next beach. Two hotsprings can be found bubbling from the rocks in this area, and a few marginally indented sandy landing areas provide good, secluded picnic spots. Near mile 1, an offshore boulder serves as a diving platform for local children.

Beach #2 is found between mile 1 and 1.5 at Posada Concepción. An RV park and houses share this beach, which is currently marked "private."

Punta Tordillo, or "Dapple-gray Point," forms a wide, cliffy stretch of coast, with the tiny Isla Coyote (or Isla Liebre) just offshore.

Beach #3, just past Punta Tordillo, is called Playa Escondido, or "Hidden Beach." Primitive campsites are available here, and the facts that the beach is smaller and a bit more difficult to see from the road improve your chance of finding it empty.

Beach #4, Playa Los Cocos is found at mile 2.5 next to a small lagoon. Shade palapas and a trash can are the only amenities here. This beach seems popular with Mexican families. Between Los Cocos and the next beach is a cacti-and-scrub valley, folded between two rocky hills.

Beach #5, Playa El Burro, has some RVs and palapas. The southern boundary of the bay is a rocky point at mile 4. The end of the point is double-lobed and shaped like a giant whale tail. At the same time, a large boulder on the southern side of the point is shaped like a whale tail in miniature. I'm not sure which of these two features inspired the name of the point: Punta Cola de Ballena.

Colorful fish are in abundance around Punta Cola de Ballena. According to Walt Peterson in his *Baja Adventure Book*, there is also an airplane wreck 200 yards off this point in 2 fathoms.

Bahía Coyote is a large bay with many sailboats anchored at its mouth, just opposite Isla Bargo (or Isla Coyote). The bay is double-coved, with two beaches. Beach #6 at mile 4.5 is marked "private" and lined with houses, RVs and palapas. Beach #7 at mile 5 is public and permits camping.

From here, Highway 1 heads inland for 10 miles and the coastline rises, becoming rockier, sheerer and less accessible by road. A series of three points follow Bahía Coyote. The first is unnamed, the second is Punta Ojitos Negros, and the third is Punta Enramada. Proceeding east along these points, you are leaving the sheltered waters of the inner bay, which encompasses the area from Playa Santispac to Bahía Coyote. Use caution.

Santa Barbara is a secluded embayment near mile 6.5. Some sailboats anchor here, but the shore inside the bay is largely undeveloped. Lush mangroves extend for most of the shore, except for beach #8, a small sand beach shaded by palm trees. A fee may be collected for camping.

Past Punta Santa Barbara, from miles 7 to 11, is a section of cliffier coast with a few rocky beaches. Expect some wave reflection and be cautious of heavy following seas, especially in winter, when strong north winds are funnelled through the mouth of Bahía Concepción.

Highway 1 meets the coast again near mile 1.5. Just past this point is San Buena Ventura, the site of beach #9, a bar-restaurant with a wooden deck and rental cabanas. The area is popular with the yachting crowd.

Finish: Playa Requesón

Playa Requesón is beach #10, at mile 12.5. The last and most unusual of the 10, this popular public beach is actually a sandspit attached to a T-shaped island, with small, sheltered coves on each side of the bar. Camping is permitted; a fee may be collected.

Playa Requesón is just off Highway 1, and easily reached if you can arrange to shuttle your car to the parking area here. Hitchhiking out is also possible.

Other Options

If you're looking for an island campsite, paddle out to Isla Bargo (Isla Coyote). Several of the other small islands have small beaches or coves, but most of them cover with high tides.

To explore more remote beaches, and to try your skills at more challenging paddling, head to the less accessible eastern shore of Bahía Concepción.

The boardwalk in downtown La Paz

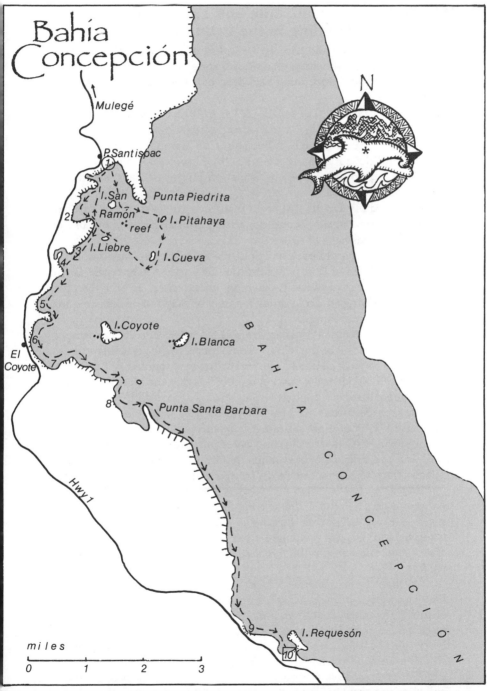

NUMBERS ALONG ROUTE LOCATE THE FOLLOWING: (1) Playa Santispac, (2) Playa Concepción, (3) Playa Escondido, (4) Playa Los Cocos, (5) Playa Burro, (6) Playa Coyote, (7) Playa (Pública) Coyote, (8) Playa Santa Barbara, (9) Playa San Buena Ventura, (10) Playa Requesón

ROUTE 13   Isla Danzante and Los Candeleros: Paddling in the Land of Giants

Trip Summary: A 19-mile trip out to and along the west side of Danzante island, through the islet chain Los Candeleros and back to Puerto Escondido, against the stunning backdrop of the Sierra de la Giganta.
Trip Length: 2 days
Charts: MEX Topo G12 C19 & G12 C29 at 1:50,000; U.S. Nautical 21141 The Moorings Chart of Isla Carmen area (see Appendix C)
Getting There: Loreto is 699 miles south of Tijuana via Highway 1. Puerto Escondido, a marina 16 miles south of Loreto, is the best place to launch for a trip to Danzante, and is just off Highway 1 at the end of a signed, paved sideroad.

There are daily flights to Loreto from Los Angeles. Buses run between Loreto and Puerto Escondido, and hitchhiking in and out of the marina is fairly easy.
Parking: You can pay to park at Tripui RV Park, just up the road from the marina facilities of Puerto Escondido. Or you can leave your car in the large lot at the marina itself; you may wish to check in with the port captain before doing so, and a small fee may or may not be collected for parking and/or launching.
Climate & Conditions: Winds are from the northwest from November to May, and the worst of the winter wind storms make paddling impossible for three days at a stretch. The rest of the year, gentler winds blow, usually from the southeast. Since winds pick up in the afternoon, early morning departures are the best strategy for easy paddling.

Winter temperatures are generally in the 70°s in the daytime, dropping to around 40° at night. Summer is blazing hot and dry, with 100°+ days the norm. In late summer and early fall, the Loreto area may get the tail-end of tropical storm systems that hit the end of the peninsula.

Sea surface temperatures range from 65° in January to 75°+ in July.

I'd driven on Highway 1 through the Sierra de la Giganta countless times. Even so, other than wincing at the sound of my car's engine wheezing and its gears grinding, I never fully appreciated the grandeur of this mountain range, which forms a spine along much of Baja California Sur.

When early missionaries visited the area, native Indians claimed that giants lived in the peaks, thus inspiring the name: "Range of the Giants." The average undersized mortal would find climbing this terraced landscape a terrifying task, especially in the region just south of Loreto where steep escarpments drop directly into the azure Cortés. But all this is difficult to imagine from the high passes of Highway 1, where a lack of perspective minimizes the sierra's height, and the only giants still prowling about are semis, barreling around the curves. To the high-

way-bound, the mountains mean little more than hairpin turns and tiring hours behind the wheel.

My first real appreciation of the Sierra de la Giganta didn't come until recently, when I first saw it from a kayak. Launching from Puerto Escondido, we paddled out to the island Danzante, its own steep, ragged profile like a sierra in miniature. Only after arriving at the western side of Danzante did we turn around to see the shore from which we'd come, and gasp.

The reddish-brown mountains on the far shore, some over 4000 feet high, seemed to be emerging directly from the sea. A local tourism campaign describes the Loreto area as a place "where even the mountains swim"; but only from a distance, from offshore, can one see how true the saying is. As the evening sea became glass, and then mirror, the jagged reflections of both Danzante and the mainland Sierra de la Giganta danced on the sea's surface. Gliding south, between the two, the reflections enveloped us. The landscape resembled the Grand Canyon, if the Grand Canyon were nearly filled with water, and one were lazily paddling along the south slope, gazing up from the flooded chasm. It indeed seemed like a place where giants might walk, and mortal men would be squashed like bugs.

If giants once roamed the land, they predominate now even more so in the sea. After gawking at the mountains, my partner and I were treated to the slow-motion appearance of the great, dark shape of a whale rising out of the water and then descending again, almost dreamlike, with barely a ripple. We scrambled for a camera and paddled quickly to the spot, saw the whale emerge a second time, panicked and fumbled to snap a picture without luck and then were left floating on mirror again, dumbstruck, with no further sign of any behemoth. We paddled an hour more, set up an island campsite with an unbeatable view, and though feeling quite small and insignificant, slept soundly.

Starting Point: Puerto Escondido

The story of Puerto Escondido is the story of modern, developing Baja: big plans, big rumors, and little results. The "big plan" was for the Mexican government tourism agency, FONATUR, to turn Puerto Escondido into a major resort, with moorings for hundreds of yachts, five-star hotels, private condos, shops, and various other places for tourists to spend money. The "big rumors" are more complicated, involving frequent changes in managers and investors and the disappearance of some money. As Puerto Escondido now stands, there have been some successful developments. One of these is that there is now a charge to launch from the port. Few services go along with this charge; though many boats do anchor here, and there are a parking lot, several build-

The Deportes Blazer sporting-goods store in Loreto: kayaks are beginning to show up all over Baja

ings, and a yacht-rental company called "The Moorings." As for the other development plans, I'm not sure where they stand, though a brisk and business-minded American seems to have taken the helm. As a kayaker with no need for a condo or a five-star hotel room, I can only wish him moderate luck.

Just up the road from the marina is Tripui RV Park, which has the most convenient tent sites, laundry facilities and restaurant for a kayaker planning an early morning launch, though the general atmosphere at Tripui leaves something to be desired. Less pretentious, though also less clean and less convenient, is Playa Juncalito, a public beach and campsite just north of Puerto Escondido on the way to Loreto.

Concrete boat launches are in plain view at Puerto Escondido. For a more discrete launch, try the tiny rocky beach opposite the "waiting room" the outer part of the harbor) just between the garbage hutch and the marina office. Strong currents reportedly run through the narrow entrance of this nearly enclosed harbor, but I have never felt them. I have noticed speedboats that don't cut their engines until the very last moment, however, so use caution. As you paddle out of the harbor, the southern part of Danzante and the islets "Los Candeleros" will be in view.

Isla Danzante

From the mouth of the harbor to Punta Coyote, the easternmost point of land sheltering the harbor, is 1 mile. A light tower and cobble landing area are at this point. From Punta Coyote to the northern tip of Danzante is a crossing of 2 miles (about a 40-minute paddle). Strong winter winds from the north can make the crossing choppy, but otherwise the area between Danzante and the mainland is fairly sheltered.

The northern tip of Danzante is only barely connected by a sandbar, which uncovers at low tide and makes for a good landing and snorkeling spot. From this sandy spot, one can also look out to the eastern side of Danzante, and watch for whales; among them blue, fin, Minke and Bryde's whales that cavort in the waters south of Isle Carmen (the enormous island looming just northeast of Danzante). Another giant that has been seen in this area is the whale shark, which isn't a whale at all but the world's largest fish. The huge, harmless plankton eater is up to 80 feet long and spotted, and often swims just under the surface.

Looking back in the direction of Puerto Escondido, one can see why it's named "Hidden Port"; the rock formations along its eastern side make it practically impossible to distinguish from sea.

The entire western shore of Danzante is less than 4 miles long. South of the sandbar, the three or four beaches along Danzante are mainly cobbles and pebbles, with small patches of coarse, salt-and-pepper-colored sand. The ridge that forms the island is very steep, so these few beaches don't extend very far back. A tent site must be carefully sandwiched between the water line and, not more than 10 or 15 feet away, scrub and cactus which blanket the rising slopes of the interior. Be careful around the jumping cholla, a type of cactus whose spiny nubs break off and act like a very painful version of velcro. The intimate and picturesque qualities of Danzante's campsites make up for the threat of unneighborly vegetation.

The first campsite is at the back of a small, three-lobed cove at mile 3.5, just south of the sandbar at Danzante's northern tip. This cove is occasionally used as a sailboat anchorage. The remaining few beaches are formed at the bases of arroyos, along the southern half of Danzante.

Camping on southern Danzante is a good way to divide up a 2-day trip, since the islets to the south are best explored in the flat seas of early morning.

All along Danzante, particularly at dawn and dusk, when the water is at its calmest, one can view wrasses, angelfish, and sergeant majors (the latter is yellow with five black vertical stripes) without needing to don snorkel gear. Students from California universities have visited Danzante to do studies on the abundant fish.

A flat rock lies offshore from the southern tip of Danzante, and the submerged reef southeast of this rock is a good area for both snorkeling and fishing.

Los Candeleros and Ensenada Blanca

The relative distances of the islets can be hard to distinguish from this point. The closest islet has no name. The middle islet is called Isla Las Tijeras, The Scissors, so named because the islet is fissured into two parts. The last islet is called Isla Pardo, which means dark or drab.

The islets are spaced about a mile apart and all three have enough of a level foreshore to permit landing in moderate weather. Each has slightly different vegetation, with a variety of brush and several species of cacti.

Southwest of Isla Pardo is Punta Estuche, visible as a dark rocky overhang. Ensenada Blanca, just inside the point at mile 11, has a narrow rim of silty, dark-yellow sand beach, backed by scrubby hills. Sailboaters occasionally anchor here, camping is possible, and a good-sized fish camp sits under shade trees at the northern end of the bay.

Return to Puerto Escondido

North of Ensenada Blanca is the Playa Ligui, a long stretch of sand-and-gravel beach interrupted by bluffs at three points. At mile 13, a low sandbar off the northern part of Playa Ligui creates a small breaker line at the shallows. Running aground is not dangerous but it certainly could be wet; just as you're trying to get dislodged from the sand the next small set of waves could easily dump you.

Two offshore islets lie north of Playa Ligui. The first, Las Islitas, at mile 14, is actually two small islets connected by a sandbar that covers at high tide. The second, Islote Blanco, at mile 15, is white with a sheerly angled side and a small rock off its southeast side. Except for a scattering of cacti, Islote Blanco looks like the Prudential Rock.

The mainland shore for the last 4 miles is fairly flat and nondescript. The mountains which hugged the shore further south move inland here, except for a few low peaks just south of the harbor mouth. You arrive back at Puerto Escondido at mile 19.

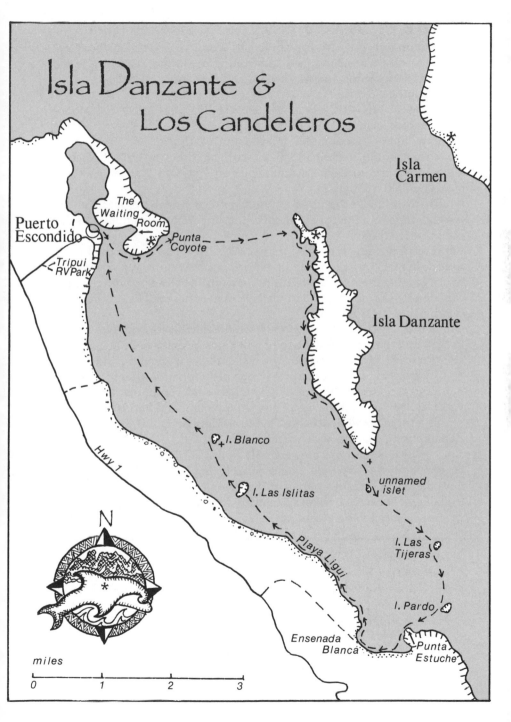

Isla Danzante &
Los Candeleros

Isla
Carmen

Puerto
Escondido

The
Waiting
Room

Punta
Coyote

Tripui
RV Park

Isla Danzante

Hwy 1

I. Blanco

I. Las Islitas

unnamed
islet

Playa Ligui

*I. Las
Tijeras*

I. Pardo

Ensenada
Blanca

Punta
Estuche

N

miles

0   1   2   3

ROUTE 14   Isla Carmen: The Abandoned Island

Trip Summary: A 59-mile trip out to and around mountainous Isla Carmen, site of a non-abandoned salt-mining operation; featuring isolation, excellent fishing and snorkeling, and challenging paddling.

Trip Length: 4–6 days.

Charts: MEX Topo G12 C19 at 1:50,000; U.S. Nautical 21141; The Moorings Chart of Isla Carmen area (see Appendix C)

Getting There: Loreto is 699 miles south of Tijuana via Highway 1. Puerto Escondido, a marina 16 miles south of Loreto, is the best place to launch for a trip to Carmen, and is just off Highway 1 at the end of a signed, paved sideroad.

There are daily flights to Loreto from Los Angeles. Buses run between Loreto and Puerto Escondido, and hitchhiking in and out of the marina is fairly easy.

Parking: You can pay to park at Tripui RV Park, just up the road from the marina facilities of Puerto Escondido. Or you can leave your car in the large lot at the marina itself; you may wish to check in with the port captain before doing so, and a small fee may or may not be collected for parking and/or launching.

Climate & Conditions: Winds are from the northwest from November to May, and the worst of the winter wind storms make paddling impossible for three days at a stretch. The rest of the year, gentler winds blow, usually from the southeast. Since winds pick up in the afternoon, early morning paddling is crucial. High north wind conditions are aggravated by the fact that the area between the mainland and Isla Carmen acts as a funnel, and the channel between Carmen and Danzante experiences strong currents year-round.

Winter temperatures are generally in the 70°s in the daytime, dropping to around 40° at night. Summer is blazing hot and dry, with 100°+ days the norm. In late summer and early fall, the Loreto area may get the tail end of tropical storm systems that hit the end of the peninsula.

Sea surface temperatures range from 65° in January to 75°+ in July.

Isla Carmen is big. Nineteen miles long, with an area 30 times that of its southwest neighbor, Danzante, it has peaks that exceed 1000 feet and valleys that stretch inland for miles. Despite its great size and nearness to the peninsula, Carmen's population is small, however: a few vagrant Mexican fishermen; some mice, bats, lizards and birds. It's a lonely place.

The orientation of the island is such that as you paddle north, you veer farther and farther away from the mainland. Paddling around the club-shaped northern head of Carmen, you lose sight of all but the highest peaks of the mainland sierra, and even these become camouflaged as they blend with the backdrop of Carmen's own russet peaks. Farther and farther you follow Carmen as she extends northeast into the Sea of Cortés; the offshore waters deepen, the cliffs at the shoreline become progressively more sheer, and when you finally pull up into a village with buildings and scattered boat parts and piers, you find it deserted: a ghost town. On 110° days, when the heat shimmers and the coast blurs into one rocky, scorched, forlorn monolith, you wonder if you'll ever see Loreto again.

Isla Carmen is challenging, and for many intimidating, but also beautiful. Each hour of paddling here is rewarded with new vistas: pastel-tinted bluffs and limestone caves, striated cliffs and, beneath one's bow, startling cobalt waters. Short of heading out to Isla Ángel de la Guarda, a far more dangerous trip, where else can one be so alone on such a large desert isle, and see so much? There is little written about Carmen, and my partner and I paddled past much of her shore without investigating it fully. The determined explorer could no doubt find the remains of villages and fish camps, old trails and arroyo niches unmarked and unmentioned in any guidebook's pages.

Starting Point: Puerto Escondido

For more background on the development, accommodations and services of Puerto Escondido and nearby Tripui RV park, see the Isla Danzante and Los Candeleros route above.

Concrete boat launches are in plain view at Puerto Escondido. For a more discrete launch, try the tiny rocky beach opposite the "waiting room" (the outer part of the harbor) just between the garbage hutch and the marina office. As you paddle out of the harbor, the southern part of Danzante will be in view.

Crossing to Carmen via Danzante

From the mouth of the harbor to Punta Coyote, the easternmost point of land sheltering the harbor, is 1 mile. A light tower and cobble landing area are at this point. From Punta Coyote to the northern tip of Danzante is a crossing of 2 miles (about a 40-minute paddle). Strong winter winds from the north can make the crossing choppy, but otherwise the area between Danzante and the mainland is fairly sheltered.

The northern tip of Danzante is only barely connected by a sandbar, which uncovers at low tide. You may want to land here for a rest and/or a snorkel, or you may paddle around the northern tip and continue on to Carmen.

The second part of the crossing, between Danzante and Carmen, is trickier. Both tidal currents and winds are funneled between Carmen and the mainland. Even on calm days, one can feel one's kayak being pushed and pulled by the troubled waters that converge, refract around and race between the islands. Although the crossing is short, it isn't recommended in strong north wind conditions.

Clockwise around Carmen

A lattice light tower perched on a sandy shore is visible on the island's southwest point, Punta Arena. Just west of this, near mile 5, is a pebbly beach that doesn't extend very far back but permits landing. Offshore boulders dot the coastline for the next 1.5 miles; after you round an unnamed point, the remainder of Carmen's long western shore finally comes into view.

Several small caves perforate the light-colored bluffs in this area. Marquer Bay, at mile 8, is divided into a small cobble and a larger gravel beach which can be used for camping. The beaches are unexceptional, but great snorkeling just offshore makes this a good spot to stop and strap on mask and fins.

The cobalt hue of the waters off western Carmen is most pronounced where the seabed is composed of barren, chalky white boulders. From below the surface, the area looks like a granite basin or pool, filled with water of stunning clarity and the additional dazzle of multicolored parrotfish, angelfish and sergeant majors. Visibility is 60–80 feet in summer, and 30–50 feet in winter. Those who prefer to stay in their kayaks can still make out great numbers of fish swimming undisturbed beneath their paddlestrokes.

Continuing up the coast between miles 9 and 15, the shoreline is fairly straight and steep, indented by only the most marginal coves. Rocky points alternate with these shallow indentations. Each rocky point has a slightly different faint tint; red, then white, then green. Just past each of the points are small cobble-and-pebble beaches. All along the way, natural formations in the rocky bluffs appear: reddish rock turrets, sienna cathedral spires. Between these formations ragged clefts provide tenuous footholds for cardon cacti and elephant trees.

At mile 15, the coast angles sharply northeast. At mile 17.5 a narrow entrance leads into a horseshoe-shaped cove, Puerto Balandra. This cove, ringed by steep bluffs and well-sheltered from winds, is a popular anchorage and is often visited by fishing boats out of Loreto. The waters are turquoise, and a narrow band of sand rings the sides of the cove. Toward the back, there are two mangrove-rimmed lagoons; between these an old trail leads into the heart of the island and over to Bahía Salinas, on the eastern side. Burros used to transport salt over this trail, and anyone who actually has energy after 17.5 miles of paddling (and adequate water and supplies) can valiantly re-enact the wearying hike.

North of Puerto Balandra, the coast is increasingly cliffy for the next 2 miles. At mile 19.5 Isla Cholla, a small, flat-topped islet sits just offshore. The islet supports a lattice light tower and one small shack; a rock reef is northwest of the islet.

The northern coast of Isla Carmen

The unnamed point across from Isla Cholla is the first of several large, prominent points which form Carmen's club-shaped head. The other points are Tintorera, Lobos and Perico. Fishing is legendary here, highlighted by continual runs of migrating yellowtail and tuna. According to Tom Miller's *Angler's Guide to Baja California*, early July in this area provides the best fishing anywhere in Mexico for big dorado.

Just around the point opposite Isla Cholla, the coastline becomes more varied. The bluffs here are very low, flat-topped and grassy, with rolling hills extending inland. From this point, one can make out Punta Tintorera, the red, rocky cliff arm jutting into the sea 4 miles to the northeast. Between these two points is a wide, moderately shallow bay.

The shore between these two points is composed of gradually rising bluffs, showing white, sheared-off sections with lime-colored streaks. A sandy stretch of shore near mile 21 is marked on one map "Deserted Village," though I haven't personally gone ashore there. A beach backed by sand dunes is just past mile 22. A sea cave is visible just before Punta Tintorera.

Punta Tintorera is a towering point at mile 23.5, with multicolored striations of lime, dark green, gold and white against a background of porous, dark red rock. Rounding it one immediately sees Punta Lobos in the distance, another bluffy, multicolored point. Between Puntas Tintorera and Lobos, the coast continues to be steep and rocky. A respite is provided at mile 25 where a broad, fairly unsheltered bay, Puerto de la Lancha, forms a pocket in the shore. Beyond the bay is a level valley that penetrates inland to the salt ponds and Bahía Salinas, farther south.

Continuing past Puerto de la Lancha there is a smaller, more hidden and sheltered V-shaped cove at mile 26. With steep, chalky white bluffs flanking its eastern perimeter (these provide a good landmark for locating the cove) and a level sandy foreshore at its narrow head, this cove makes a picturesque stopping point. Here too, one map marks this area "Deserted Village."

Many small caves invite exploration as one proceeds along the coast. A large offshore rock marks mile 27.5. A narrow channel is formed between the rock and the shore, and sequestered under overhangs and niches in this area are the telltale crates and half-hidden gear of local fishermen.

The very tip of Punta Lobos is actually a cluster of steep rocks connected to the arm of the point by a long sandbar. A light tower is poised on the southern shore of the sandbar, visible after you've rounded the point. Strong wave refraction can occur around this point, and from here south to Punta Perico is a 7-mile stretch of unsheltered, sheer cliff coast with few good stopping or camping spots, heavy wave reflection and even some dumping surf in marginally pocketed spots along the cobble-and-boulder foreshore. Except for Punta Perico, the cliffy point at the end of this stretch, there are few landmarks, only moderate variations in the barren, fissured escarpments looming above.

Waves strike heavily on Perico Point at mile 35, sending geysers of spray billowing from a large rock just off the tip of the point in heavy seas. Continuing around the point, you paddle northwest into the broad embrace of wide-mouthed Salinas Bay. The bay is not very sheltered, since the level valley extending behind it enables wind to sweep down from the north, and the wide mouth of the bay is open to winds from the southeast and south. A red-and-white striped light tower is visible on the eastern shore of the bay.

The waters of the bay are very shallow, and flat sandy terrain forms the bay's head and the now-abandoned site of an old salt-mining village at mile 38. Many remote parts of the Baja coast have a haunted, half-deserted air, and it is common to come upon a single old shack or a crumbling foundation, but the village at Bahía Salinas is remarkable because entire houses, buildings and pieces of equipment are still in place. A salt barge sunk in the middle of the harbor area can be seen poking above water level. A few vagrant fishermen have staked out sleeping spaces in the hulls of rusting ships and other strange spots, but otherwise the village is empty.

This ghost town, so forlorn and seldom visited now, once had quite worldly connections. According to a historical note in the book *Island Biogeography in the Sea of Cortez*, the Russian colony at Sitka, Alaska, was dependent on salt purchased at Carmen Island for the preservation of furs. In 1841 a Russian scientist was on board when the ship Naslednik Aleksandr stopped at the island to pick up the colony's salt supply. During his trip, which include several other stops in the gulf, the scientist succeeded in gathering 360 plant specimens, which are now housed in the Komarov Botanical Institute of the Academy of Sciences, St. Petersburg.

Proceeding south from Bahía Salinas, the coastline resumes its cliffy profile. There are no bays or deep coves along Carmen's east side south of Bahía Salinas; any small coves, niches or beaches are formed by arroyos. The first of these is just south of White Point, at mile 41, just past a cluster of offshore rocks. Two other small niches can be found at miles 45 and 46.5.

Past cliffy Colorado Point at mile 48, the coastline decreases in elevation, flattening out to dwarf bluffs and the flat, sandy southeast point, Punta Baja. The southeast reaches of Isla Carmen are not as spectacular as the north ones, but due to their nearness to Puerto Escondido they are more frequently visited. A camping spot on Punta Baja would be a good place for whalewatching; blue and fin whales are common here.

After rounding Punta Baja, at mile 52, one proceeds for 2 more miles to Punta Arena (site of a light tower) and retraces one's route across to the northern tip of Danzante and the harbor at Puerto Escondido, finishing the route at mile 59.

Other Options

Many kayakers who come to Carmen don't circumnavigate the entire isle, preferring to combine a shorter exploration of Carmen's southern tip with a trip to Danzante.

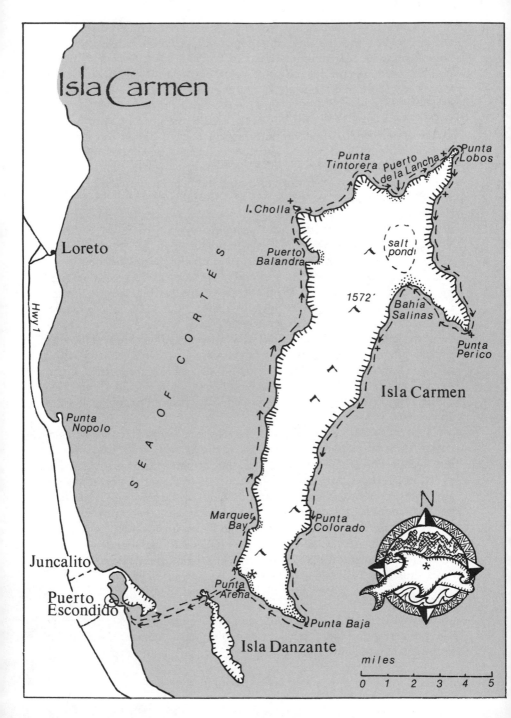

Isla Carmen

Loreto

Punta Tintorera

Puerto de la Lancha

Punta Lobos

I. Cholla

Puerto Balandra

salt pond

1572'

Bahía Salinas

Punta Perico

SEA OF CORTÉS

Isla Carmen

Hwy 1

Punta Nopolo

Marquer Bay

Punta Colorado

Juncalito

Puerto Escondido

Punta Arena

Isla Danzante

Punta Baja

N

miles
0   1   2   3   4   5

ROUTE 15   Isla Espíritu Santo: The Pearl of the Cortés

Trip Summary: A 35-mile circumnavigation of a stunning, semi-tropical island with white-sand beaches, towering bluffs, and numerous secluded caves. A 4-mile crossing to and from the island contributes to a total of 43 miles for the trip; challenging paddling with ample reward.

Trip Length: 4–6 days.

Charts: MEX Topo G12 D62, G12 D63, G12 D72, G12 D73 at 1:50,000; U.S. Nautical 21120

(Reportedly, few charts/maps of this island are highly accurate.)

Getting There: La Paz, Baja California Sur's capital city, is 922 miles south of Tijuana via Highway 1; the city is also served by several airlines. The beaches ½ hour north of La Paz are the starting point for trips to Isla Espíritu Santo. Follow the city's main thoroughfare, Paseo Alvaro Obregón, as it turns into MEX Highway 11 and heads for 10 miles to the beaches Pichilingue, Balandra and Tecolote (all signed). Tecolote, currently the end-of-the-line for Highway 11, faces north with a view of the island.

Parking/Shuttle Logistics: Since this route doesn't actually begin in the city of La Paz, but at a satellite beach to the north, a little extra prelaunch planning is required.

There is no place to leave one's car securely at Tecolote. Any car left parked for several days here, or at the other beaches, may be considered "abandoned" by police and could be confiscated. Two options are public parking lots in La Paz (inquire at the tourism office) and leaving the car at a hotel or trailer park with permission. Unfortunately, all of these places are quite far from Tecolote. A little closer is the guarded lot at the ferry terminal at Pichilingue, where I have got permission to leave my car in the past.

Beach concessionaires at Tecolote are friendly and will usually keep an eye on kayaks and gear while you park your car and find your way back to the beach. Especially on weekends, traffic to and from the beach is frequent and hitchhiking is easy. Buses from downtown La Paz go at least as far as Pichilingue. Communal taxis also ply the route all the way to Tecolote.

Climate & Conditions: La Paz falls just short of being in the tropics (the Tropic of Cancer lies about 80 miles south near Santiago). Winters are balmy, with daytime temperatures in the 70°s. Summers are blazing hot, in the 90–100°s, although *coromuel* breezes cool off the city each evening in time for nightly strolls along the *malecón* (the sea wall or boardwalk). The area receives about 5 inches of rain in late summer and early fall, the same time of year that *chubascos* (tropical storms) hit the southern tip of the peninsula.

Water surface temperatures range from 68° in January to 79° in July.

Strong winds blow from the northwest from November to May, usually from about 9 a.m. to 4 p.m. These winds sweep down both sides of the island. The rest of the year, winds are from the southeast or southwest. An additional complication is the *coromuel*, which blows each summer evening from the south (and, in my experience, seems to keep blowing all night and even into early morning). Jack Williams, author of the *Baja Boater's Guide*, adds that whether or not they qualify as *coromuels*, nighttime breezes from the south are occasionally experienced in winter as well.

Recommended Reading: Bring a copy of John Steinbeck's *The Pearl*, inspired by his visit to this area.

"Piratas?" the city librarian repeated dubiously, one eyebrow cocked. She scanned the dusty history books on the shelves, turned up the fan, cast a weary glance toward the few library patrons who sat at dark tables, rustling through newspapers. "No, no. Pirates? Not in La Paz." With that she dispatched us. We left the library, stumped again, dodging taxis and taco vendors in our search for a little history, a glimpse into this now-bustling city's past.

Given the way that La Paz has so wholeheartedly embraced its modern role as a capital city, that past is a little hard to find. Was this really the place where mutineer Fortún Jiménez and his crew landed in 1533, only to be killed by natives for trying to rape the women and loot the pearls of La Paz Bay? Was this the place that Cortés landed in 1535, lured by the rumors of those same pearls? Were there really once Indians here, who according to one missionary dove for pearls from their dugout canoes, suffering great headaches, until by the fifth day their ears bled? Were there really pirates who hid in the natural harbors here, waiting out hurricane season and hiding from Spanish ships?

What is difficult to find in dusty libraries, and even more difficult to imagine with one's own eyes, can still be found in words, anecdotes and place names. Take Pichilingue Bay, for instance, the modern site of the ferry terminal and public beach. The word "pechelingue" was an old term for pirate, derived from the name of the home port of Flemish free-booters: Vlissingen. The word for the southerly summer breeze, coromuel, may be a corruption of the name of the pirate Cromwell, who in legend sailed out with the southerly late afternoon breeze and returned the next day with the northwesterlies. The kayaker has much to learn from local legend.

But is one left with only these tantalizing hints of a more exotic past?

With our romantic visions unsatisfied, we headed for Tecolote, to start our kayak trip; there, we discovered an amazing thing. Though the summer crowds throng, and the traffic of La Paz spills all the way over to this small beach, it stops there. Espíritu Santo Island, just across the channel, seems to be in its own world; in the past, perhaps.

"My grandfather found skulls, human skulls, in a cave on one of the peaks there," a Mexican man told us, pointing to the island.

"Pirates?" I asked.

He smiled. "Well, there have been stories of treasure, of gold ..."

Once on the island, Holy Spirit Island as it is called, we began to imagine legends for ourselves. Caves dot the southeast shore, and striated cliffs loom farther up the east side, obscuring the island's interior. On the west, there are at least 13 coves, each one of them a perfect hiding place for pirates, waiting for well-heeled yachties to pass by and be snared. In one cove, we found the foundation of an old building, which a fishermen told us had once been part of a pearling operation.

Here, away from the noise and bustle of La Paz, one could easily imagine Indians in dugout canoes, conquistadors appearing on the horizon out of the coppery haze of sunset, and treasures being wrested from the sea.

And where there were no pirates, or legends waiting to be discovered, we nonetheless found incredible beauty. Espíritu Santo has some of the finest beaches in Baja, the eeriest multi-hued bluffs, and the most alluring campsites, guarded by high, cacti-studded slopes and backed by thickly vegetated arroyo valleys.

We left the island only after our food, water and time ran out. From a remote beach on Espíritu Santo, where only two of us had shared a wide stretch of white sand, we crossed back over to Tecolote on the mainland, where perhaps a hundred people all huddled on no larger a beach.

We laughed to think of the dubious, scowling librarian in La Paz. Far from the city, we'd found what we were seeking—perhaps not pirates or authentic treasure, but certainly the most beautiful pearl the Cortés has to offer.

Starting Point: Tecolote Beach, La Paz

La Paz is a bustling, proud, modern city of 150,000 with a wide range of accommodations, excellent restaurants, tourist services, and more ice cream shops and seafood taco stands than perhaps any other city in Baja. Of special interest to the kayaker: Deportiva La Paz, at 1680 Obregón, sells snorkel and scuba gear. A few hotels, including the Hotel Perla, currently offer panga-escorted kayak and/or snorkel trips to Los Islotes, the small islets just off Espíritu Santo.

Playa Tecolote, or "Owl Beach," was once reachable only by sturdy, 4-wheel-drive vehicles. Now, a good road leads directly from La Paz to Tecolote, approximately 15 miles north. Several marisco stands serving clam, oyster and various other seafood cocktails are set up on the beach, and jet-skis and boats can be rented (including small, squarish, wooden boats called *cayucos*—hmmm . . .)

If you thought beach culture was limited to upper California, think again. Though sedate during the week, Tecolote explodes on weekends. Mexican families turn out in droves to play volleyball, eat ceviche, rumble around on motorbikes and generally have a colorful, chaotic, good time. The best timing is to leave Tecolote early in the week, guaranteeing a low-profile launch, and return on the weekend when you're ready to celebrate your completed trip.

The owner and staff of the Playa Azul, a mariscos stand to the right as you enter Tecolote, have been very helpful in the past. I've had luck chartering a very inexpensive panga over to Espíritu Santo (carrying kayaks, camping gear and all). This service is up to the individual kayaker to arrange on an informal basis, but worth considering if you'd rather have more time on the island and less en route.

Crossing from Tecolote

The crossing is just under 4 miles. Between Tecolote and the island, the waters in this area are shallow, bisected by a slightly deeper 1-mile-wide channel, the Canal de San Lorenzo, through which most large boat traffic passes. The limits of this channel are marked by two structures: a tall metal structure on Scout Shoal to the south, and a smaller buoy on San Lorenzo Reef to the north (see map). Crossing from Tecolote to Punta Lupona, you should keep both structures on your right.

Given the shallowness of the entire area, the water does not seem to get as whipped up as one might expect. Nonetheless, be cautious of strong winds from the northwest as well as quick-moving currents through the channel in winter months. Generally, I have found the crossing quite easy in calm weather, but chose a panga lift one particularly windy day.

Orientation to Espíritu Santo (and Partida)

Espíritu Santo is a large, topographically unusual island, and there is no one way to see it. Flat, sandy shores make up the southern extremity, tall cliffs predominate along the eastern side, the Isla Partida sits like a tophat to the north, extending the perimeter of the combined islands by a third, and sheltered coves lure sailboats and kayaks on the western side. Obviously, to see it all—to contrast the stark, looming profile of the east with the tranquil, pocketed shoreline of the west—one must do a circumnavigation of Espíritu Santo and Partida. The route below is designed for just that.

Just as enjoyable, however, would be a more leisurely exploration of the western sides of both islands. The waters to the west are calmer, and there are more camping sites and more places to land quickly if winds spring up or fatigue threatens.

A third option would be to circumnavigate Espíritu Santo without including Isla Partida, the island just to the north that is essentially an extension of Espíritu Santo. In other words, paddle north along the east side, but cross over about two-thirds of the way via the Caleta Partida, a cove that actually divides Espíritu Santo from Isla Partida, and continue south along the west side back to your starting point.

In any case, consider the route below as merely a way of describing the island, not as an itinerary. Exploring one small part of the island fully might be just as rewarding as zipping all the way around it. Total mileage on this trip will vary extremely, even if you follow the route described, based on whether you investigate every cove, how close you keep to shore, and so on. The trip miles in the route are estimates only.

Finally, in addition to being flexible about your mileage, stay flexible about your direction. I describe Espíritu Santo and Partida in a counterclockwise direction, the best (in my mind) if winds are blowing regularly from the southeast or southwest. When winds are from the northwest, on the other hand (usually November–May), the reverse direction may be preferable. In any case, if doing a full circumnavigation, keep in mind that the eastern side is the more challenging, and plot your direction with the current season's prevailing winds in mind.

Southeastern/Eastern Espíritu Santo

Punta Lupona is a low, sandy point on the southern side of Espíritu Santo, fronted by shimmering, turquoise shallows. A fine rim of white sand extends along most of the shore to Punta Bonanza, interrupted by a few low-profile, rockier areas. Swimming is wonderful here (though remember to shuffle your feet to warn off any stingrays), the water is particularly warm, and landing and launching are easy.

You may notice a small shack east of Punta Lupona, or crates and cutting blocks dusted with salt behind the beach just past the point. These are used by Mexican fishermen, who clean, salt and dry *manta rayas* (actually mobulas) caught off the island for market in peninsular Baja.

Punta Bonanza, 2 miles from Punta Lupona, is a rocky point fronted by a small shoal. Some rocks protrude above water level in this area. The sand rim continues a short distance beyond Punta Bonanza, but then the coastline gets rockier and its elevation increases, bluffs and some small caves appearing above the water line along the shore.

At mile 5, near Punta Lobos, the waters just offshore deepen considerably, the bluffs on shore steepen, and wave reflection becomes increasingly noticeable. Exposed boulders just offshore contribute to turbulence when waves get choppy. The bone-white bluffs in this area, coarsely fissured, look like giant molars or shattered vertebrae, and contribute to an eery, stark ambience on this less visited side of the island.

Just past Punta Lobos is a bay with a few rocky landing spots. On the northern side of this bay is an uncharted inland lagoon.

From an unnamed point at mile 8, the cliffs steepen further and begin to display horizontal striations of red, orange, white and black. Even though there are no sheltered coves between here and Caleta Partida, there are a few cobble landing areas. Less comfortable than any beaches on the west side, these cliff-ringed sites are nonetheless remarkable for their isolation and rugged beauty. Snorkeling in the rocky areas offshore is excellent, hiking and rock climbing are possible, and few sailboats dare to anchor here, thereby ensuring campers' privacy.

The last miles to Caleta Partida reveal more stunning coastline. The striated cliffs give way to bluffs topped by high caps of blond sandstone, sculpted and pockmarked, and veined with ochre. The deep waters off the eastern side of the island are known for runs of yellowtail in winter and spring, and yellowfin tuna in summer and fall, as well as sailfish and billfish, which might be a little difficult to land from the cockpit of a kayak.

Near the very northeast corner of Espíritu Santo, there is a cave large enough for paddlers to enter. Large sally lightfoot crabs, their shells lacquered red, purple and black, skitter along the rocks inside the cool, dark cave.

At mile 13, Caleta Partida separates Isla Espíritu Santo from its northern neighbor, Isla Partida. The cove, or channel, is somewhat S-shaped, and can be navigated by kayak or panga. Two small fish camps lie inside the cove. Anchoring boats favor this area, and it may be crowded; nonetheless, it is a possible camping site. One may paddle westward to shortcut over to the western side of Espíritu Santo, or skip the channel and continue north to circumnavigate Partida.

Isla Partida

The eastern side of Partida is composed of sheer, dark cliffs. At least one cobble landing breaks up the 4-mile stretch. Refracting waves can be quite strong along and around the northern extremity of Partida.

Los Islotes, two small, steep islets north of Partida, become visible at mile 17. A lattice light tower sits on the flattened top of the larger islet to the west. Boats ferry snorkelers and divers out to the islets, giving clumsily outfitted humans the chance to swim, swerve and roll around underwater with the far more agile sea lions that live on Los Islotes. Kayakers are at a disadvantage, since making a landing on the rocks that are the sea lions' home is prohibited. Plunging overboard from a dive boat, anchored offshore, is easier and less disruptive. If you do head out to the islets just to paddle, remain at last 75 feet offshore, and

Fissured cliffs on the east side of Isla Espíritu Santo

be wary of aggressive males (sea lions, not sailboaters) during the May–August breeding season.

Cliffs continue around the northern point of Partida, until near mile 18 one enters the first of 13 coves. Embudo is a tiny, shallow cove with glowing, aqua waters and a sand beach, most of which is taken up by fish-camp apparatus: drying lines, boxes, a single shack, makeshift storage bins hiding under rock overhangs. Only the fishermen themselves were missing when I pulled into Embudo. A few names and drawings etched into a half-hidden rock made the cove seem particularly private; my partner and I quickly paddled away to find a campsite where we would be less intrusive.

The coloration of the bluffs past Embudo varies from blond sandstone striped with red and green, to tan and orange bluff topped by crumbly black rocks. Small sea caves and arches also vary the steep shoreline. A small islet sits offshore, just before the entrance of Ensenada Grande, a large, three-lobed cove at mile 19. Each of the three lobes is backed by a fine-sand beach, and your choice of a campsite may depend on where the day's yachts have anchored.

Exploring on land in this cove and the many that follow, you may notice some of the wildlife that inhabits Espíritu Santo and Partida. In addition to a large variety of sea- and shorebirds, there are twenty species of reptiles and amphibians, and six of mammals. The mammals are particularly curious: there is a black-tailed jackrabbit, endemic to Espíritu Santo, as well as one species of ground squirrel, two of mice, one rat and a ring-tailed cat that is a skinny relative of the raccoon. A ring-tailed cat tried to make off with our cooking pot one night while we were camping in Ensenada Grande. After a startled yip and a scuttle for the flashlight, we scared the animal off and sat back down around our campfire, laughing at the ring-tail's audacity. We were even more startled the second time, when it returned to try to retake the pot right in front of our eyes.

A small, unnamed, two-lobed inlet is just south of Ensenada Grande. Just past it is a long, broad cove, El Cardonal, which penetrates deeply into Partida, nearly cleaving it in two. At the back of Cardonal are two beaches: a better sand one to the north separating a jutting hill from a mangrove-backed beach to the south. A lagoon and a level valley sit at the back of this long cove and make for good inland exploring.

Cardonalcito, or "Little Cardonal," is a particularly scenic cove at mile 23. A sand beach at the back of the small cove is flanked by tall, cactus-studded red-rock bluffs; the Baja image of desert looming so close to the sea is typified here. Behind the beach, a short, level trail leads to an old well. The water can be used for portable showers, but bring your own bucket.

Caleta Partida is accessible again at mile 24, this time from the western side, and it forms the southern boundary of Isla Partida.

Western Espíritu Santo

Mesteño, or "Untamed," Cove is small, ringed by steep bluffs, and backed by a fine-sand beach.

Caleta El Candelero, or "Candlestick Cove," is a medium-sized cove, guarded from its center by a finely fissured islet called the Roca

Monumento. A navy building is visible on the sand beach at the back of the cove, and an old well lies inland.

Isla Ballena, or "Whale Island," sits offshore from a cove of the same name, at mile 28. Caleta Ballena has a wide, white-sand beach. From here south, the hills above the shore take on a gentler appearance, often tinged with green scrub. Points between the coves continue to exhibit interesting sandstone formations, such as Punta Raza, just south of Caleta Ballena, where sandstone shelves jut just above water level from the bases of bluffs.

Puerto Ballena is a bay divided into three smaller coves by two steep, rocky ridges. The ridges rise above water level to reappear offshore as two small islets, Gallo and Gallina ("Rooster" and "Hen"). The best beach is to be found on the north face of the second, more southerly ridge, in the middle cove; this beach may be used by local fishermen to clean their catch, however. Mangroves cover most of the shore within Puerto Ballena, and there are surprisingly few good camping sites given the bay's large size. The foundations of a building from pearling days can be found on the southern shore of the third cove; the beach here is made of sharp, white coral.

A small, unnamed cove is at mile 31. At mile 32.5, the shore dips in to form a large, extremely shallow bay, the Bahía San Gabriel. A coral reef can be found on the north side of the bay. A small, two-lobed, unnamed cove is the last one on the island's western side.

Punta Dispensa, at mile 34, can be identified by a large red mound that sits inland and slightly east of the point. Rounding Punta Dispensa, one paddles into the area of shallow azure waters and wide, white-sand beach that characterize the island's southern extremity. Punta Lupona is at mile 35.

Finish: Tecolote Beach

Be wary of following seas on the return crossing, especially in winter months when winds blow from the northwest. San Lorenzo Reef and the Scout Shoal structures should be on your left as you paddle back to the peninsula. Tecolote can sometimes be spotted from the sea by looking for the glinting of cars traveling the last stretch of road to the beach. This applies mainly to weekends, however. If returning in midweek, you'll be far more dependent on compass readings.

On the very last stretch, as the marisco-stand umbrellas and volleyball nets come into view, use caution: you wouldn't want to get run over by a 14-year-old on a jet-ski after surviving a 43-mile paddle around a desert isle. Enjoy the curious stares as you make landfall and amble up to Playa Azul to request your well-deserved octopus cocktail.

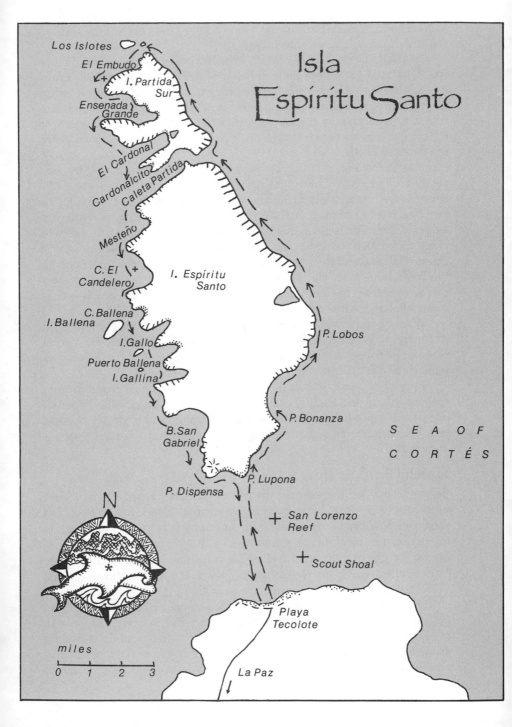

Isla
Espíritu Santo

Los Islotes
El Embudo
I. Partida
Sur
Ensenada
Grande
El Cardonal
Cardonalcito
Caleta Partida
Mesteño
C. El
Candelero
I. Espíritu
Santo
C. Ballena
I. Ballena
I. Gallo
Puerto Ballena
I. Gallina
P. Lobos
B. San
Gabriel
P. Bonanza
SEA OF
CORTÉS
P. Dispensa
P. Lupona
San Lorenzo
Reef
Scout Shoal
N
Playa
Tecolote
miles
0   1   2   3
La Paz

Appendices

Appendix A   **Tours and Rentals**

Organizations offering tours and rentals are subject to change. To find the latest listings, check out advertisements and special vacation sections in magazines like *Sea Kayaker*, *Canoe*, and *Outside*.

Most tours listed below do not require previous kayaking experience. The similarities stop there, however. Some tours provide a fully catered, carefully orchestrated trip complete with panga escorts and expert chefs. Others stress a more self-sufficient, expedition-style approach. Ask lots of questions before you make your reservation.

Baja Expeditions
2625 Garnet Avenue
San Diego, CA 92109
(619) 581-3311 (619) 581-6542 FAX
Probably the biggest and best known of the kayak tour companies, Baja Expeditions offers 9-day trips to Isla Espíritu Santo from October to June, and to Magdalena Bay from January to March. Pangas provide escort, carry all luggage, and provide opportunities for close encounters with whales (Magdalena Bay) or sea lions (Isla Espíritu Santo).

Baja Tropicales
Box 60
Mulegé, B.C.S.
México 23900
011-526-853-0019
3-03-63 FAX
From a palapa on the shore of Playa Santispac, just south of Mulegé, Baja Tropicales offers kayak mini-excursions under the guidance of Roy Mahoff and Becky Aparicio. Personalized instruction and local ecology are emphasized. The most popular trip is a half-day "paddle, snorkel, dive and dine" which allows kayakers to gather their own shellfish for a post-paddle feast.

Baja Tropicales also rents out kayaks to experienced paddlers; phone, fax or write for more information.

Deportes Blazer
Hildalgo No. 18
Loreto, B.C.S., México
011-526-833-0006
They don't offer tours, but they do rent kayaks—a few, at least. This
Loreto sports store is sorely lacking in accessories, instruction, etc., but
if you're looking for a bare-bones, on-the-spot rental, try calling or stop-
ping by.

Elakah! Expeditions
P.O. Box 4092
Bellingham, WA 98227
(206) 734-7270
Elakah offers 10-day sea kayak and overland trips to Bahía de Los
Ángeles. Kayakers paddle 3–7 miles per day. Both coed and women's
trips are offered; minimum-impact touring is assured.

National Outdoor Leadership School
Box AA
Lander, WY 82520
(307) 332-6973
NOLS offers kayaking trips, as well as longer wilderness and leadership
courses that include backpacking and sailing. Call or write for more information.

Paddling South
4510 Silverado Trail
Calistoga, CA 94515
(707) 942-4796 (June–September)
(707) 942-4550 (October–May)
Paddling South has been operating since the "early '80s." Trudi Angell
and accompanying trip leaders take kayakers on 7–10 day trips in the
Loreto area, paddling 5–10 miles a day. Free time and flexibility are
stressed.

Seaquest Expedition
Zoetic Research
P.O. Box 2424
Friday Harbor, WA 98250
(206) 378-5767
SeaQuest promises a true "expeditionary-style" trip, without motor-
ized support pangas. Biologists accompany kayakers on 5- or 7-day
trips.

Southwest Sea Kayaks
1310 Rosecrans St.
San Diego, CA 92106
(619) 222-3616

Southwest Sea Kayaks offers the widest range of Baja trips, specializing in regular excursions and weekenders for those who have their own kayaks as well as those wanting to rent. Trips have included San Quintín Bay, La Bufadora and Santo Tomás, Bahía de Los Ángeles, Islas Encantadas; and, for the hardcore paddler, Isla Ángel de la Guarda. A regular newsletter announces adventures in the planning.

Southwest Sea Kayaks also rents kayaks to experienced paddlers. For the inexperienced, there are basic lessons, roll and rescue clinics, evening paddles and more to prepare you for a future trip.

Tofino Expeditions
114-1857 West 4th Ave.
Vancouver, B.C. V6J 1M4
(604) 737-2030
(604) 737-7348 FAX

From February to April, Tofino Expeditions takes kayakers on 8-day trips in the Mulegé/Bahía Concepción area. Paddling takes up 3–4 hours each day, with time left over for snorkeling and swimming.

Ron Yarnell Wilderness: Alaska/Mexico
1231 Sundance Loop
Fairbanks, AK 99709
(907) 479-8203
(907) 452-1821

January trips to Isla Espíritu Santo and Magdalena Bay are offered. Both trips last 8 days, with kayakers paddling 5–8 miles on "moving days."

Appendix B   Recommended Reading

About Kayaking

Burch, David, *Fundamentals of Kayak Navigation*. Chester, CT: Globe Pequot Press. 1987.

Dowd, John, *Sea Kayaking: A Manual for Long Distance Touring* (2nd ed.). Seattle: University of Washington. 1988.

Evans, Eric and Jay Evans, *The Kayaking Book* (2nd ed.). Lexington, MA: Stephen Greene Press. 1988.

Washburne, Randel, *The Coastal Kayaker's Manual: A Complete Guide to Skills, Gear and Sea Sense*. Chester, CT: Glove Pequot Press. 1989.

About Baja

Anon., *Baja California*. Los Angeles: Automobile Club of Southern California. 1990. (The "AAA" guide)

Cannon, Ray, *The Sea of Cortez*. Menlo Park, CA: Lane Books, 1966.

Case, Ted J., and Martin L. Cody, eds., *Island Biogeography in the Sea of Cortez*. Berkeley: University of California Press. 1983.

Fons, Valerie, *Keep It Moving: Baja by Canoe*. Seattle: The Mountaineers. 1986.

Franz, Carl, *The People's Guide to Mexico*. Santa Fe, NM: John Muir Publications. 1972.

Gotshall, Daniel W., *Marine Animals of Baja California: A Guide to the Common Fishes and Invertebrates*. Monterey, CA: Sea Challengers. 1982.

Mackintosh, Graham, *Into a Desert Place*. Idyllwild, CA: Graham Mackintosh. 1988.

Miller, Tom, *Angler's Guide to Baja California*. Huntington Beach, CA: Baja Trail Publications. 1987.

Peterson, Walt, *The Baja Adventure Book* (2nd ed.). Berkeley: Wilderness Press. 1992.

Steinbeck, John, and Edward R. Ricketts, *The Log from the Sea of Cortez*. New York: Viking Press. 1941.

Steinbeck, John, *The Pearl*. New York: Viking Press. 1947.

Wayne, Scott, *Baja California: A Travel Survival Kit*. Berkeley: Lonely Planet Publications. 1988.

Wilbur, Sanford R., *Birds of Baja California*. Berkeley: University of California Press. 1987.

Williams, Jack, *Baja Boater's Guide*, vols. I & II. Sausalito, CA: H. J. Publications, 1988.

Related Reading

Forgey, William W., *Wilderness Medicine*. Merrillville, IN: ICS Books. 1987.

Fox, William T., *At the Sea's Edge: An Introduction to Coastal Oceanography for the Amateur Naturalist*. New York: Prentice Hall Press. 1983.

Jones, Mary Lou, Steven L. Swartz and Stephen Leatherwood, eds., *The Gray Whale: Eschrichtius robustus*. Orlando, FL: Academic Press. 1984.

Appendix C   Addresses For
                   Ordering Maps And Charts

The following businesses carry a wide range of Baja-related material,
including Mexican topographical maps, U.S. nautical charts, tide tables,
and books of interest to the Baja kayaker. Call or write for map/chart
indices and catalogs.

Baja Explorer Topographic Atlas Directory
P.O. Box 81385
San Diego, CA 92138-1385
(800) 669-2252 Extension A

Map Centre, Inc.
2611 University Avenue
San Diego, CA 92104-2894
(619) 291-3830
(619) 291-3840 FAX

The Moorings
1305 U.S. 19 South, Suite 402
Clearwater, FL 34624
(800) 535-7289
(They sell a chart of the Isla Carmen area)

New York Nautical Instruments
140 West Broadway
New York, NY 10013
(212) 962-4522

University of Arizona
Publishing Support Services
102 West Stadium
Tucson, AZ 85721
(602) 621-2571
(602) 621-6478 FAX

Wide World of Maps
2626 W. Indian School Road
Phoenix, AZ 85017
(602) 279-2323

Appendix D   Beaufort Scale

Beaufort Number	Seaman's description of wind	Velocity m.p.h.	Estimating velocities on land	Estimating velocities on sea	Probable mean height of waves	Description of Sea
0	Calm	Less than 1	Smoke rises vertically	Sea like a mirror		Calm (glassy)
1	Light Air	1-3	Smoke drifts; wind vanes unmoved.	Ripples with the appearance of scales are formed but without foam crests.	1/2	Rippled
2	Light breeze	4-7	Wind felt on face; leaves rustle; ordinary vane moved by wind	Small wavelets, still short but more pronounced; crests have a glassy appearance. Perhaps scattered white caps.	1	Smooth
3	Gentle breeze	8-12	Leaves and twigs in constant motion; wind extends light flag.	Large wavelets. Crests begin to break. Foam of glassy appearance. Perhaps scattered whitecaps.	2-1/2	
4	Moderate breeze	13-18	Raises dust and loose paper; small branches are moved.	Small waves, becoming longer, fairly frequent white caps.	5	Slight
5	Fresh breeze	19-24	Small trees in leaf begin to sway; crested wavelets form on inland water.	Moderate waves, taking a more pronounced long form; many white caps are formed. (Chance of some spray.)	10	Moderate
6	Strong breeze	25-31	Large branches in motion; whistling heard in telegraph wires; umbrellas used with difficulty.	Large waves begin to form; the white foam crests are more extensive everywhere. (Probably some spray.)	15	Rough
7	Moderate gale	32-38	Whole trees in motion; inconvenience felt in walking against wind.	Sea heaps up and white foam from breaking waves begins to be blown in streaks.	20	Very Rough
8	Fresh gale	39-46	Breaks twigs off trees; generally impedes progress.	Moderately high waves of greater length; edges of crests break into spindrift. The foam is blown in well-marked streaks along the direction of the wind.	25	High
9	Strong gale	47-54	Slight structural damage occurs.	High waves. Dense streaks of foam along the direction of the wind. Sea begins to roll. Spray may affect visibility.	30	
10	Whole gale	55-63	Trees uprooted; considerable structural damage occurs.	Very high waves with long, overhanging crests. The surface of the sea takes a white appearance.	35	Very high
11	Storm	64-73		The sea is completely covered with long white patches of foam lying along the direction of the wind. Everywhere edges of the wave crests are blown into froth. Visibility affected.	40	
12	Hurricane	74-82		The air is filled with foam and spray. Sea completely white with driving spray; visibility very seriously affected.	45 or more	Phenomenal

Index

Acknowledgements

To the friends, family members, fellow kayakers and kind acquaintances who have supported us in our ventures, both on land and at sea, thank you:

C. Romano & Jay Zarzana, Honorée Romano, John Cress, Evelyn & Louis Lax, Amy Bower, Matt Garcia, Thom Veratti, Roy Mahoff, Becky Aparicio, the residents of Puertecitos, the residents of Gonzaga Bay, Mari and Cliff Hurley, Marie Woods, the Gordon & Johnson clan, Dan Breedon, Fran, Grant, James Boxall, Nick the Greek (San Francisco), Graham MacKintosh, Daniel Anderson, Mike Finkel, Rachel Elson, Jeff Creath, the staff of Erehwon in Bannockburn, and the Chicago Canoe Base; and, last but not least, Thomas Winnett at Wilderness Press for his patience and assistance.

Special thanks to Liz Romano, who gallantly braved quick-mud, cramped living conditions, short tempers, incredible heat and humidity, and endless *huevos rancheros* on our most recent research trip.

Special thanks to the captain and crew of *Estado 29*, who provided not only emergency assistance but also the finest hospitality and shipboard dining we have ever experienced in Baja.

And final thanks to everyone who fed us, drove us, sheltered us, humored us and provided inspiration and support along the way.

Brian R. Lax and Andromeda Romano-Lax

Born in Chicago, Illinois, over a thousand miles from the nearest ocean, Andromeda Romano-Lax had no interest in sea kayaking until she visited Mexico's Baja Peninsula. Originally interested in Mexican politics and culture (she earned a B.A. in Political Science), she became particularly intrigued by the coast of the Sea of Cortés. Her desire to visit Baja's remote coastal communities and fishing camps prompted her to consider kayaking the coast. Though neither had ever kayaked before, she managed to talk a new acquaintance, Brian Lax, into accompanying her. Subsequent trips blossomed into a passion for kayaking, a marriage, and this book, *Sea Kayaking in Baja*, for which she wrote the text and made the maps, and he took the pictures and provided all-around support.

Romano-Lax now lives in a small fishing village in Nova Scotia, Canada with her husband and dog. She is pursuing a Master's degree in Marine Management at Dalhousie University. Once wary of the sea, she now hopes that responsible tourism and recreational sea kayaking can play a role in education and the conservation of marine environments.

Sea Kayaking in Baja
1995 Update

Route 7, Gonzaga Bay

In 1994, facilities at Alfonsina's were being expanded. A new airplane runway, enlarged cantina and increased fresh-water supplies have been reported by visitors.

Route 8, Bahía de Los Ángeles

A reader, Derek Lane, commented on the growing problem of shark carcasses littering many of the islands' beaches, spoiling otherwise fine kayaking and camping trips.

Appendix A

New tour group listing:
Ecosummer Expeditions
P.O. Box 8014-240
936 Peace Portal Drive
Blaine, WA 98230
In U.S.A. 1-800-688-8605
In Canada 1-800-465-8884
(604) 669-3244 FAX

Ecosummer Expeditions has been operating sea kayaking trips in Baja since the early '80s. From January to March, 7-day trips in the Pacific lagoons feature whale- and bird-watching. Also offered in the spring is a more challenging 14-day trip along the steep, rugged coast between Loreto and La Paz. Ask about their sail-rigged kayaks if you've been wanting to try something new.

Appendix A

Phone/FAX number change:
Baja Tropicales' new (1994) FAX number is 011-52-115-3-01-90.

Appendix B, Recommended Reading About Baja:

Cummings, Joe, *Baja Handbook*. Chico, CA: Moon Publications. 1993.

Appendix C

New map/chart company:
Sea of Cortez Cruising Charts
P.O. Box 976
Patagonia, AZ 85624
(602) 394-2393

(With the help of Ed Gillet of Southwest Sea Kayaks, Gerry Cunningham is publishing a new series of paddle charts. The first covers the Bahía de Los Ángeles area south to San Francisquito. The second will cover Bahía Concepción to Islas Carmen and Danzante.)

READ THIS

The descriptions in this guidebook are necessarily cast in general terms. Neither the descriptions nor the maps can be assumed to be exact or to guarantee your arrival at any given point. You must undertake only those trips and trip segments that you know are within your competence.

Given these cautions, you can have a wonderful time in Baja.